£1·50

£1.

Georg Lukács

NLB

Lenin

A Study on the Unity
of his Thought

First published by
Verlag der Arbeiterbuchhandlung, Vienna, 1924
© Hermann Luchterhand Verlag GmbH, 1967
Translated by Nicholas Jacobs
This translation first published 1970
© NLB, 1970

NLB, 7 Carlisle Street, London W1

Designed by Gerald Cinamon
Typeset in Monotype Ehrhardt by
Western Printing Services Ltd, Bristol
SBN 902308 00 9

Foreword 7

Publisher's Note: *Some notes have been added on personalities and events where their significance is not apparent from the text and is important for an understanding of it. Notes have not been included on such well-established figures as Bernstein, Kautsky and Martov.*

Foreword

The following short account does not for a moment claim to deal in any way exhaustively with the theory and practice of Lenin. It is merely an attempt – in rough outline – to show the relationship between the two, written in the belief that it is precisely this relationship which is not clearly enough in evidence, even in the minds of many Communists. Not only would thorough treatment of all these problems require considerably more space than these few pages; there is also not nearly enough material available for such an account of Lenin's life-work, particularly for those to whom the relevant Russian literature is only accessible in translation. The story of Lenin's life must be set in the historical framework of at least the last thirty to forty years. Let us hope a study worthy of the task is soon available. The author of these introductory remarks is himself deeply aware of how difficult it is to write about individual problems before the totality of which they form part has been clarified – to popularize before what is to be popularized has been established with incontestable scholarship. For this reason no attempt has been made to present the problems which occupied Lenin's life either in their entirety or in the exact order in which they occurred. Their selection, sequence, and development are dictated exclusively by the desire to make their interrelationship stand out as clearly as is conceivably possible. The quotations, too, are selected on this basis and not on one of chronological accuracy.

Vienna, February 1924

1. The Actuality
of the Revolution

Historical materialism is the theory of the proletarian revolution. It is so because its essence is an intellectual synthesis of the social existence which produces and fundamentally determines the proletariat; and because the proletariat struggling for liberation finds its clear self-consciousness in it. The stature of a proletarian thinker, of a representative of historical materialism, can therefore be measured by the depth and breadth of his grasp of this and the problems arising from it; by the extent to which he is able accurately to detect beneath the appearances of bourgeois society those tendencies towards proletarian revolution which work themselves in and through it to their effective being and distinct consciousness.

By these criteria Lenin is the greatest thinker to have been produced by the revolutionary working-class movement since Marx. Opportunists, unable either to deny or ignore his importance, vainly say that Lenin was a great political figure in Russia, but that he lacked the necessary insight into the difference between Russia and the more developed countries to become leader of the world proletariat. They claim that his historical limitation was that he generalized uncritically the problems and solutions of Russian reality and applied them universally. They forget what is today only too rightly forgotten: that the same accusation was also made, in his time, against Marx. It was said that he formulated his observations of English economic life and of the English factory system uncritically as general laws of all social development; that his observations may in themselves have been quite correct but, precisely because they were distorted into general laws, they became incorrect. It is by now unnecessary to refute this error in detail and show that Marx never 'generalized' from particular experiences limited in time and space. On the contrary – true to the methods of genuine historical and political genius – he detected, both theoretically and historically, in the microcosm of the English factory system, in its social premisses, its conditions and consequences, and in the historical trends which both lead to, and in turn eventually threaten its development, precisely the macrocosm of capitalist development as a whole.

For, in science or in politics, this is what sets the genius apart from the mediocre scholar. The latter can only understand and differentiate between immediately given, isolated moments of the social process. When he wants to draw general conclusions he in fact does nothing more than interpret as 'general laws', in a truly abstract way, certain aspects of phenomena limited in time and space, and apply them accordingly. The genius, on the other hand, for whom the true essence, the living, active main trends of an age are clear, sees them at work behind every event of his time and continues to write about the decisive basic issues of the whole epoch even when he himself thinks he is only dealing with everyday affairs.

Today we know that this was Marx's greatness. From the structure of the English factory system he identified and explained all the decisive tendencies of modern capitalism. He always pictured capitalist development as a whole. This enabled him to see both its totality in any one of its phenomena, and the dynamic of its structure.

However, there are today only few who know that Lenin did for our time what Marx did for the whole of capitalist development. In the problems of the development of modern Russia – from those of the beginnings of capitalism in a semi-feudal absolutist state to those of establishing socialism in a backward peasant country – Lenin always saw the problems of the age as a whole: *the onset of the last phase of capitalism and the possibilities of turning the now inevitable final struggle between bourgeoisie and proletariat in favour of the proletariat – of human salvation.*

Like Marx, Lenin never generalized from parochially Russian experiences limited in time and space. He did however, with the perception of genius, immediately recognize the fundamental problem of our time – the approaching revolution – at the time and place of its first appearance. From then on he understood and explained all events, Russian as well as international, from this perspective – from the perspective of the actuality of the revolution.

The actuality of the revolution: this is the core of Lenin's thought and his decisive link with Marx. For historical materialism as the conceptual expression of the proletariat's struggle for liberation could only be conceived and formulated theoretically when revolution was already on the historical agenda as a practical reality; when, in the misery of the proletariat, in Marx's words, was to be seen not only the misery itself but also the revolutionary element 'which will bring down the old order'. Even at that time it was necessary to have the undaunted insight of genius to be able to see the actuality of the proletarian revolution. For the average man first sees the proletarian revolution when the working masses are already fighting on the barricades, and – if he happens also to have enjoyed a vulgar-Marxist education – not even then. For to a vulgar Marxist, the foundations of bourgeois society are so unshakeable that, even when they are most visibly shaking, he only hopes and prays for a return to 'normality', sees its crises as temporary episodes, and regards a struggle even at such times as an irrational and irresponsible rebellion against the ever-invincible capitalist system. To him, the fighters on the barricades are madmen, the defeated revolution is a mistake, and the builders of socialism, in a successful revolution – which in the eyes of an opportunist can only be transitory – are outright criminals.

The theory of historical materialism therefore presupposes

the universal actuality of the proletarian revolution. In this sense, as both the objective basis of the whole epoch and the key to an understanding of it, the proletarian revolution constitutes the living core of Marxism. Despite this delimitation, expressed in the absolute rejection of all unfounded illusions and in the rigorous condemnation of all putschism, the opportunist interpretation of Marxism immediately fastens on to the so-called errors of Marx's individual predictions in order to eliminate revolution root and branch from Marxism as a whole. Moreover, the 'orthodox' defenders of Marx meet his critics half way: Kautsky explains to Bernstein that the question of the dictatorship of the proletariat can quite easily be left to the future – to a very distant future.

Lenin re-established the purity of Marxist theory on this issue. But it was also precisely here that he conceived it more clearly and more concretely. Not that he in any way tried to improve on Marx. He merely incorporated into the theory the further development of the historical process since Marx's death. This means that the actuality of the proletarian revolution is no longer only a world historical horizon arching above the self-liberating working class, *but that revolution is already on its agenda.* It was easy for Lenin to bear the accusations of Blanquism, etc., which this position brought him, not only because he was in good company – for he had to share these accusations with Marx (with 'certain aspects' of Marx) – but because he had well and truly earned his place alongside such company. On the one hand, neither Marx nor Lenin ever thought of the actuality of the proletarian revolution and its aims as being readily realizable at any given moment. On the other hand, however, it was through this actuality that both gained a sure touchstone for evaluating all questions of the day. The actuality of the revolution provides the key-note of a whole epoch. Individual actions can only be considered revolutionary or counter-revolutionary when related to the central issue of revolution, which is only to be discovered by an accurate analysis of the socio-historic whole. The actuality of the revolution therefore implies study of each individual daily problem in concrete association with the socio-historic whole, as moments in the liberation of the proletariat. The development which Marxism thus underwent through Lenin consists merely – merely! – in its increasing grasp of the intimate, visible, and momentous connexion between individual actions and general destiny – the revolutionary destiny of the whole working class. It merely means that every question of the day – precisely as a question of the day – at the same time became a fundamental problem of the revolution.

The development of capitalism turned proletarian revolution into an everyday issue. Lenin was not alone in seeing this revolution approaching. However, he stood out not only by his courage, devotion and capacity for self-sacrifice from those who beat a cowardly retreat when the proletarian revolution they had themselves acclaimed in theory as imminent became an actuality. His theoretical clarity also distinguished him from the best, most dedicated and far-sighted of his contemporaries. For even they only interpreted the actuality of the revolution as Marx had been able to in his time – as the fundamental problem of the period as a whole. From an exclusively universal point of view, their interpretation was correct. They were, however, incapable of applying it and using it to establish firm guide-lines for all questions on the daily agenda, whether they were political or economic, involved theory or tactics, agitation or organization. Lenin alone took this step towards making Marxism, now a quite practical force, concrete. That is why he is in a world historical sense *the only theoretician equal to Marx* yet produced by the struggle for the liberation of the proletariat.

2. The Proletariat as the Leading Class

The instability of conditions in Russia had become apparent long before the real development of capitalism there, long before the existence of an industrial proletariat. Already much earlier, the break-up of agrarian feudalism and the decay of bureaucratic absolutism had not only become undeniable facts of Russian reality but had led to the formation of strata which rose up from time to time against Tsarism, even if still in an ill-defined, confused, and merely instinctive way – to peasant unrest and radicalization of the so-called de-classed intelligentsia. Clearly, the development of capitalism, however much its actual existence as well as its significance remained obscure to even acute observers, sharply heightened the objective confusion and its revolutionary ideological consequences. In the second half of the nineteenth century it must have been increasingly obvious that Russia, in 1848 still the secure refuge of European reaction, was gradually developing towards revolution. The only question was: what would be the character of this revolution? And, closely allied to this: which class should play the leading role in it?

It is easy to understand why the first generation of revolutionaries were extremely unclear as to how to pose such questions. They saw in the groups which rose up against the Tsar first and foremost a homogenous element: the people. The division into intellectuals and manual workers was clear even at this stage. But it was not of decisive importance because there could only be very ill-defined class outlines among 'the people', while only really honest revolutionaries among the intellectuals joined the movement – revolutionaries who regarded it as their implacable duty to merge themselves with 'the people' and represent only its interests.

Yet even at this stage of the revolutionary movement, the developments in Europe were bound to impinge on events and therefore to effect the historical perspective from which the revolutionaries evaluated them. Here the question automatically arose: was the European course of development, the development of capitalism, the inescapable fate of Russia as well? Must Russia too pass through the capitalist hell before finding salvation in socialism? Or could she, because she was unique, because of her still-existent village communes, by-pass this stage and find a path from primitive direct to developed communism?

The answer to this question was by no means as obvious then as it seems to us now. Had not Engels still answered it in 1882 by saying that if a Russian revolution simultaneously produced a European proletarian revolution, 'then the system of communal property in today's Russia can serve as a point of departure for the development of communism'?

This is not the place even to outline the disputes fought over this issue. It simply forces us to choose our starting-point, because with it arose the question: which was to be the leading class of the coming revolution in Russia? For it is clear that the recognition of village communism as its point of origin and economic foundation necessarily makes the peasantry the leading class of social transformation. And, corresponding to this difference from Europe in its economic and social basis, the revolution would have to look for other theoretical foundations than historical materialism, which is no more than the conceptual expression of the necessary transition of society from capitalism to socialism under the leadership of the working class. The argument as to whether Russia is in the process of developing along capitalist lines – whether Russian capitalism is capable of development – further, the theoretico-methodological controversy as to whether historical materialism is a generally valid theory of social development and, finally, the discussion centring on which class in society is called upon to be the real motive force of the Russian revolution – all turn on the same question. They are all ideological reflections of the evolution of the Russian proletariat – moments in the development of its ideological (and corresponding tactical, organizational) independence from other social classes.

This is a protracted and painful process through which every labour movement must pass. Only the individual problems in which the particularities of the class situation and the autonomy of the class interest of the proletariat express themselves constitute its specifically Russian element. (The German working class was at a comparable stage in the Lassalle-Bebel-Schweitzer period and German unity constituted one of its decisive problems.*[1]) But a correct solution to precisely these local problems *as such* must be found if the proletariat as a class is to win its independence of action. The best theoretical training is absolutely worthless if it limits itself to generalities: to be effective in practice it must express itself by solving precisely these particular problems. (Wilhelm Liebknecht, for example, although a passionate internationalist and direct pupil of Marx, was by no means able more often or more reliably to make the right decisions than the Lassalleaner,[2] who were much more confused on a purely theoretical level.) But what is further peculiar to Russia here is that this theoretical struggle for the independence of the proletariat, for the recognition of its leading role in the coming revolution, has nowhere found so clear and unequivocal a solution as precisely *in* Russia. Thus, the Russian proletariat was to a great extent spared those hesitations and regressions to be found in the experience of all the developed countries without exception – not in the course of successful class struggle where they are unavoidable, but in theoretical clarity and in tactical and organizational confidence. At

*Numbers refer to the Notes on p. 103.

least its most conscious stratum was able to evolve, theoretically and organizationally, as directly and as clearly as its objective class situation had evolved from the economic forces of Russian capitalism.

Lenin was not the first to take up this struggle. But he was alone in thinking through every question radically to its very end: in radically transforming his theoretical insight into practice.

Lenin was only one among other theoretical spokesmen in the fight against 'primitive' Russian socialism, against the Narodniks. This was understandable: his theoretical struggle aimed to establish the independent and leading role of the proletariat in determining the fate of Russia. However, because the course and substance of this argument could only consist in proving that the typical path taken by capitalist development as outlined by Marx (i.e. primitive accumulation) was also valid for Russia – that a viable capitalism could and must exist there – this debate perforce brought the spokesmen of proletarian class struggle and the ideologists of nascent Russian capitalism temporarily into one camp. For the theoretical differentiation of the proletariat from the amorphous mass of 'the people' by no means automatically brought with it the knowledge and recognition of its independence and leading role. On the contrary, the simple, mechanistic, undialectical logic of the proof that the developmental tendencies of the Russian economy pointed in the direction of capitalism appeared to be the unqualified acceptance and promotion of its approach. This was true not only for the progressive bourgeoisie whose – temporarily – 'Marxist' ideology is readily understandable when it is borne in mind that Marxism is the only economic theory which demonstrates the inevitability of the rise of capitalism from the decomposition of the pre-capitalist world. It must appear even more necessary to all 'proletarian' Marxists who have interpreted Marx mechanistically instead of dialectically; who do not understand what Marx learnt from Hegel and incorporated in his own theory, freed from all mythology and idealism: that the recognition of a fact or tendency as actually existing by no means implies that it must be accepted *as a reality constituting a norm for our own actions*. It may be the sacred duty of every genuine Marxist to face the facts squarely and without illusions, but for every genuine Marxist there is always a reality more real and therefore more important than *isolated* facts and tendencies – namely, *the reality of the total process*, the totality of social development. Hence, Lenin writes: 'The bourgeoisie makes it its business to promote trusts, drive women and children into the factories, subject them to corruption and suffering, condemn them to extreme poverty. We do not "demand" such development, we do not "support" it. We fight it. But *how* do we fight? We explain that trusts and the employment of women in industry are progressive. We do not want a return to the handicraft system, to pre-monopoly capitalism, domestic drudgery for women. Forward through trusts, etc., and beyond them to socialism!'

This provides the standpoint for the Leninist solution to this whole range of questions. It follows that the recognition of the necessity of capitalist development in Russia and of the historical progress implicit in this development by no means compels the proletariat to support it. The proletariat must welcome it, for it alone establishes the basis of its own appearance as the decisive force; but it must welcome it as *the condition and the premise of its own bitter struggle* against the real protagonist of capitalism – against the bourgeoisie.

Only this dialectical understanding of the element of necessity in historical tendencies created the theoretical space for the autonomous appearance of the proletariat in the class war. If the necessity of capitalist development in Russia is simply accepted after the fashion of the ideological pioneers of the Russian bourgeoisie and, later, the Mensheviks, it would follow that Russia must before all else complete its capitalist development. The protagonist of this development is the bourgeoisie. According to this schema, only after it has progressed a long way, after the bourgeoisie has swept away both the economic and political vestiges of feudalism and has established a modern, capitalist, democratic state in its place, can the independent class struggle of the proletariat begin. A premature appearance of the proletariat with independent class aims is not only useless, because it is barely worth considering as an autonomous force in the battle between the bourgeoisie and Tsarism, but is also disastrous for the proletariat itself. It frightens the bourgeoisie, decreases its striking power against Tsarism and drives it straight into its arms. According to this interpretation, for the time being the proletariat can only be considered an auxiliary of the progressive bourgeoisie in the struggle for a modern Russia.

It is clear today, even though it was not at the time, that this whole debate was rooted in the question of the actuality of the revolution. For those who were not more or less conscious bourgeois ideologists, paths separated according to whether the revolution was seen as a current issue on the agenda of the labour movement, or as a distant 'end goal' on which current decisions seemed unsuited to exercise any definite influence. It is indeed more than questionable whether the Menshevik position, even if its historical perspective could be considered correct, would ever be acceptable to the proletariat; whether such faithful vassals of the bourgeoisie would not obscure class-consciousness so completely that dissociation from the bourgeoisie as an independent act by the proletariat would be made ideologically impossible or at least considerably more difficult at a historical moment considered appropriate even by Menshevik theory (one need only think here of the English working class). Admittedly this is, in practice, idle speculation. The dialectic of history, which opportunists try to eliminate from Marxism, is nevertheless bound to operate on them against their will, driving them into the bourgeois camp and in their eyes postponing the independent appearance of the proletariat into the hazy distance of a virtually non-existent future.

History justified Lenin and the few who proclaimed the actuality of the revolution. The alliance of the progressive bourgeoisie, which had already proved an illusion at the time of the struggle for German unity, would only have survived if it had been possible for the proletariat as a class to follow the bourgeoisie into its alliance with Tsarism. For the actuality of the revolution means that the bourgeoisie has ceased to be a revolutionary class. No doubt, compared with absolutism and feudalism, the economic system whose protagonist and beneficiary is the bourgeoisie represents progress. But this progressive character of the bourgeoisie is again dialectical. The necessary link between the economic premises of the bourgeoisie and its demands for political democracy or the rule of law, which – even if only partially – was established in the great French Revolution on the ruins of feudal absolutism, has grown looser. On the one hand, the increasingly swift approach of the proletarian revolution *makes possible an alliance between the bourgeoisie and feudal absolutism* in which the conditions for the economic existence and growth of the bourgeoisie are secured by the political hegemony of the old ruling forces. On the other hand, *the bourgeoisie, in its ideological decadence resulting from this alliance, abandons the realization of its own former revolutionary demands to the proletarian revolution.*

However problematic this alliance between the bourgeoisie and the old ruling powers may be, since it is of course a compromise which springs from mutual fear of a greater evil and not a class alliance based on common interests, it still remains an important new fact beside which the schematic and mechanistic 'proof' of the 'necessary link' uniting capitalist development to democracy must reveal itself to be a complete illusion. 'In any case,' said Lenin, 'political democracy – even if it is in theory normal for so-called pure capitalism – is only one of the possible *forms* of the superstructure *over* capitalism. The facts themselves prove that both capitalism and imperialism develop under and in turn subjugate *any* political forms.' In Russia specifically, the reason for this swift volte-face by the bourgeoisie from a position of – apparent – radical opposition to Tsarism to support of it lies essentially in the 'inorganic' development of capitalism grafted onto Russia, which even in its origins displayed a pronouncedly monopolistic character (dominance of large-scale industry, role of finance capital). From this it followed that the bourgeoisie was a numerically smaller and socially weaker stratum there than in other countries which underwent a more 'organic' capitalist development. However, at the same time, the material foundations for the development of a revolutionary prole-tariat were laid down sooner in the large-scale factories than the purely statistical estimates of the pace of Russian capital-ist development would have suggested.

But if alliance with the progressive bourgeoisie proves illusory, and if the proletariat in its progress towards inde-pendence has already made its final break with the chaotic concept of 'the people', will it not, precisely because of this hard-won independence, be totally isolated and therefore involved in a necessarily hopeless struggle? This frequent and very obvious objection to Lenin's historical perspective would be valid if the rejection of the agrarian theories of the Narodniks, the recognition of the necessary dissolution of the vestiges of agrarian communism, were not also dialectical. The dialectic of this process of dissolution – for dialectical understanding is always only the conceptual form of a real dialectical fact – lies in the inevitability of the dissolution of these old forms only having an unambiguous, definite direction in so far as it is a process of dissolution, in other words only negatively. Its positive direction is by no means inherent in it and depends on the evolution of the social environment, on the rate of the whole historical context. Put more concretely: the economically unavoidable dissolution of the old agrarian forms – of the large as well as of the small estates – can proceed in two different ways. 'Both solutions, each in its different way,' said Lenin, 'facilitate the change to a higher stage of technology and point towards agricultural progress.' One is the sweeping-away from the lives of the peasantry of all vestiges of medieval and earlier practices. The other – Lenin called it the Prussian way – 'is characterized by the legacy of medieval landed property not being abolished all at once but gradually adapted to capitalism'. Both are possible. Compared with what existed before, both are economically progressive. But if they are both equally possible and – in a certain sense – equally progressive, what decides which of the two is destined to become reality? Lenin's answer to this question, as to any other, is clear and unambiguous: the class struggle.

Thus the outlines of the situation in which the proletariat, on its own, is called upon to play the leading role become sharper and more concrete. For the *decisive force* in this class struggle, which for Russia points the way to the transition from medieval to modern times, *can only be the proletariat*. The peasants, not only because of their extreme cultural backwardness, but above all because of their objective class position, are only capable of instinctive revolt against their increasingly intolerable situation. Because of their objective class position they are doomed to remain a politically vacillating stratum – a class whose destiny is ultimately decided by the urban class struggle, the destiny of the towns, large-scale industry, the state apparatus.

Only this context places the decision in the hands of the proletariat. Its struggle against the bourgeoisie would at a given historical moment be less promising if the bourgeoisie succeeded in abolishing Russian agricultural feudalism in its own way. The fact that Tsarism makes this difficult is the main reason for the temporarily revolutionary, or at least the oppositional, posture of the bourgeoisie. *But as long as this question remains unresolved, the elemental explosion of the enslaved and impoverished millions on the land remains a permanent possibility*: an elemental explosion to which only the proletariat can give a direction. It alone can lead this mass movement to a goal of real benefit to the peasantry, and which will create the conditions in which the proletariat can take up the struggle against Tsarism with every hope of victory.

Thus, Russia's socio-economic structure established the objective basis for the alliance of proletariat and peasantry. Their class aims were different. That is why the crude soldering together of their forces in the name of vague and populist concepts like 'the people' was eventually bound to fall apart. However, it is only by joint struggle that they can realize their different aims. Thus the old Narodnik ideas return dialectically transformed in Lenin's characterization of the Russian revolution. The vague and abstract concept of 'the people' had to be rejected, but only so that a revolutionary, discriminating, concept of 'the people' – *the revolutionary alliance of all the oppressed* – could develop from a concrete understanding of the conditions of the proletarian revolution. This was why Lenin's party justifiably considered itself the heir to the real Narodnik revolutionary tradition. But because the consciousness and ability to lead this struggle exist – in objective class terms – *only in the class-consciousness of the proletariat*, it alone can and must be the leading class of social transformation in the approaching revolution.

3. The Vanguard Party of the Proletariat

We have seen that the proletariat's historical task is both to emancipate itself from all ideological association with other classes and to establish its own class-consciousness on the basis of its unique class position and the consequent independence of its class interests. Only thus will it be capable of leading all the oppressed and exploited elements of bourgeois society in the common struggle against their economic and political oppressors. The objective basis of the leading role of the proletariat is its position within the capitalist process of production. However it would be a mechanistic application of Marxism, and therefore a totally unhistorical illusion, to conclude that a correct proletarian class-consciousness – adequate to the proletariat's leading role – can gradually develop on its own, without both frictions and setbacks, *as though the proletariat could gradually evolve ideologically into the revolutionary vocation appropriate to its class*. The impossibility of the economic evolution of capitalism into socialism was clearly proved by the Bernstein debates. Nevertheless, its ideological counterpart lived on uncontradicted in the minds of many honest European revolutionaries and was, moreover, not even recognized as either a problem or a danger. That is not to say that the best among them completely ignored its existence and importance, that they did not understand that the path to the ultimate victory of the proletariat is long and passes through many defeats, and that not only material setbacks but also ideological regressions are unavoidable on the way. They knew – to quote the words of Rosa Luxemburg – that the proletarian revolution which, because of its social

preconditions, can no longer happen 'too early', must however necessarily happen 'too early' as far as the maintenance of power (of ideological power) is concerned. But if,
despite this historical perspective of the proletariat's path of
liberation, it is still held that a spontaneous revolutionary
self-education of the masses (through mass action and other
experiences), supplemented by theoretically sound party
agitation and propaganda, is enough to ensure the necessary
development, then the idea of the ideological evolution of
the proletariat into its revolutionary vocation cannot truly
be said to have been overcome.

Lenin was the first and for a long time the only important
leader and theoretician who tackled this problem at its
theoretical roots and therefore at its decisive, practical
point: *that of organization.*

The dispute over the first clause of the party statute at
the Brussels/London Congress in 1903 is by now common
knowledge. It turned on whether it was possible to be a
member of the party merely by supporting and working
under its control (as the Mensheviks wanted), or whether it
was essential for members to take part in illegal activity, to
devote themselves wholeheartedly to party work, and to
submit to the most rigorous party discipline. Other questions of organization – that of centralization, for instance –
are only the necessary technical consequences of this latter,
Leninist standpoint.

This dispute can also only be understood in relation to the
conflict between the two different basic attitudes to the
possibility, probable course and character, of the revolution,
although only Lenin had seen all these connexions at the
time.

The Bolshevik concept of party organization involved the
selection of a group of single-minded revolutionaries, prepared to make any sacrifice, from the more or less chaotic
mass of the class as a whole. But does not the danger then
exist that these 'professional revolutionaries' will divorce
themselves from their actual class environment and, by thus

separating themselves, degenerate into a sect? Is this concept of the party not just a practical result of that Blanquism which 'intelligent' Revisionists claim to have discovered even in Marx? This is not the place to examine how far this criticism misses its mark even in relation to Blanqui himself. It misses the core of Lenin's concept of party organization simply because, as Lenin said, the group of professional revolutionaries does not for one moment have the task of either 'making' the revolution, or – by their own independent, bold actions – of sweeping the inactive masses along to confront them with a revolutionary *fait accompli*. *Lenin's concept of party organization presupposes the fact – the actuality – of the revolution*. Had the historical predictions of the Mensheviks been correct, had a relatively quiet period of prosperity and of the slow spread of demo-cracy ensued, in which – at least in backward countries – the feudal vestiges of the 'the people' had been swept aside by the 'progressive' classes, the professional revolutionaries would have necessarily remained stranded in sectarianism or become mere propaganda clubs. The party, as the strictly centralized organization of the proletariat's most conscious elements – and only as such – *is conceived as an instrument of class struggle in a revolutionary period*. 'Political questions cannot be mechanically separated from organization ques-tions,' said Lenin, 'and anybody who accepts or rejects the Bolshevik party organization independently of whether or not we live at a time of proletarian revolution has completely misunderstood it.'

But the objection could arise, from the diametrically opposite viewpoint, that it is precisely the actuality of the revolution that makes such an organization superfluous. It may have been useful to organize and unite professional revolutionaries when the revolutionary movement was at a standstill. But in the years of the revolution itself, if the masses are deeply stirred, if within weeks – even days – they undergo more revolutionary experiences and become more mature than previously in decades, if even those sections of the class who have hitherto resisted association with the movement even on questions of immediate interest to themselves become revolutionary, then such a party organization is superfluous and meaningless. It wastes needed energies and, if it gains influence, restricts the spontaneous revolutionary creativity of the masses.

This objection clearly leads back again to the problem of an evolutionary ideological development into socialism. *The Communist Manifesto* defines very clearly the relationship between the revolutionary party of the proletariat and the class as a whole. 'The Communists are distinguished from the other working-class parties by this only: 1. In the national struggles of the proletarians of different countries, they point out and bring to the fore the common interests of the entire proletariat, independently of all nationality. 2. In the various stages of development which the struggle of the working class against the bourgeoisie has to pass through, they always and everywhere represent the interest of the movement as a whole. The Communists, therefore, are on the one hand, practically, the most advanced and resolute section of the working-class parties of every country, that section which pushes forward all the others; on the other hand, theoretically, they have over the great mass of the proletariat the advantage of clearly understanding the line of march, the conditions, and the ultimate general results of the proletarian movement.' They are – in other words – *the tangible embodiment of proletarian class-consciousness*. The problem of their organization is determined by their conception of the way in which the proletariat will really gain its own class-consciousness and be itself able to master and fully appropriate it. All who do not unconditionally deny the party's revolutionary role accept that this does not happen of itself, either through the mechanical evolution of the economic forces of capitalism or through the simple organic growth of mass spontaneity. The difference between Lenin's party concept and that of others lies primarily, on the one hand, in his deeper and more thorough appreciation of the different economic shadings within the proletariat (the growth of labour aristocracy, etc.) and, on the other, in his vision of the revolutionary cooperation of the proletariat with the other classes in the new historical perspective we have already outlined. From this follows the increased importance of the proletariat in the preparation and leader-ship of the revolution and, from this in turn, the party's leadership of the working class.

From this standpoint, the emergence and increasing significance of a labour aristocracy means that the ever-present – relative – divergence between the direct day-to-day interests of specific working-class groups and those of the real interests of the class as a whole widens and even-tually petrifies. Capitalist development, which began by forcibly levelling differences and uniting the working class, divided as it was by locality, guilds, etc., now creates a new form of division. This not only means that the proletariat no longer confronts the bourgeoisie in united hostility. The danger also arises that those very groups are in a position to exercise a reactionary influence over the whole class whose accession to a petty-bourgeois living-standard and occupa-tion of positions in the party or trade union bureaucracy, and sometimes of municipal office, etc., gives them – despite, or rather because, of their increasingly bourgeois outlook and lack of mature proletarian class-consciousness – a superiority in formal education and experience in adminis-tration over the rest of the proletariat; in other words, whose influence in proletarian organizations thus tends to obscure the class-consciousness of all workers and leads them towards a tacit alliance with the bourgeoisie.

Theoretical clarity, corresponding agitation and propa-ganda by conscious revolutionary groups are not enough by themselves against this danger. For these conflicts of interest express themselves in ways which remain concealed from the workers for a long time; so much so that even their own ideological spokesmen sometimes have no idea that they have themselves already forsaken the interests of the class as a whole. Thus, these differences can very easily be hidden from the workers under the rubric of 'theoretical differences of opinion' and mere 'tactical differences', and the revolutionary instinct of the workers, which explodes from time to time in great spontaneous mass actions, is then unable to preserve such instinctive heights of active class-consciousness as lasting possessions for the class as a whole.

This alone makes the organizational independence of the fully conscious elements of the proletariat indispensable. It is this that demonstrates *that the Leninist form of organization is inseparably connected with the ability to foresee the approaching revolution.* For only in this context is every deviation from the right path fateful and disastrous for the proletariat; only in this context can a decision on an apparently trivial everyday issue be of profound significance to it; only in this context is it a life-and-death question for the proletariat to have the thoughts and actions which truly correspond to its class situation clearly in front of it.

However, the actuality of the revolution also means that the fermentation of society – the collapse of the old framework – far from being limited to the proletariat, involves all classes. Did not Lenin, after all, say that the true indication of a revolutionary situation is 'when *"the lower classes" do not want* the old way, and when *"the upper classes" cannot carry on* in the old way'? 'The revolution is impossible without a complete national crisis (affecting both exploited and exploiters).' The deeper the crisis, the better the prospects for the revolution. But also, the deeper the crisis, the more strata of society it involves, the more varied are the instinctive movements which criss-cross in it, and the more confused and changeable will be the relationship of forces between the two classes upon whose struggle the whole outcome ultimately depends: the bourgeoisie and the proletariat. *If the proletariat wants to win this struggle, it must encourage and support every tendency which contributes to the break-up of bourgeois society, and do its utmost to enlist every upsurge – no matter how instinctive or confused – into the revolutionary process as a whole.* The approach of a revolutionary period is also heralded by all the dissatisfied elements of the old society seeking to join, or at least to make contact with, the proletariat. But precisely this can bring with it hidden dangers. If the proletarian party is not organized so that the correct and appropriate class policy is assured, these allies – who always multiply in a revolutionary situation – can bring confusion instead of support. For the other oppressed sections of society (peasants, petty-bourgeoisie, and intellectuals) naturally do not strive for the same ends as the proletariat. The working class, provided it knows what it wants and what its class interests dictate, can free both itself and these other groups from social bondage. But if the party, the militant representative of proletarian class-consciousness, is uncertain of the direction the class should take, if its proletarian character is not even institutionally safeguarded, then these other groups will stream into it and deflect it from its path. Their alliance, which would have benefited the revolution if the proletarian party had been sure of its class organization, can then instead be the greatest danger to it.

Lenin's idea of party organization therefore contains as fixed poles: the strictest selection of party members on the basis of their proletarian class-consciousness, and total solidarity with and support for all the oppressed and exploited within capitalist society. Thus he dialectically united exclusive singleness of purpose, and universality – the leadership of the revolution in strictly proletarian terms and its general national (and international) character. The Menshevik concept of party organization weakened both these poles, confused them, reduced them to compromises, and united them *within the party itself*. The Mensheviks shut themselves off from broad strata of the exploited masses (for example, from the peasants), but united in the party the most diverse interest groups, thus preventing any homogeneity of thought and action. During the chaotic

mêlée of the class struggle – for all revolutionary periods are characterized by the deeply disturbed, chaotic state of society as a whole – instead of helping to establish the *proletarian unity against the bourgeoisie so essential for victory*, and of rallying other hesitant oppressed groups to the proletariat, a party so organized becomes a confused tangle of different interest groups. Only through inner compromise does it ever manage to take any action and, even then, either follows in the wake of the more clear-minded or more instinctive groups within it, or remains forced to look on fatalistically while events pass it by.

Lenin's concept of organization therefore means *a double break with mechanical fatalism*; both with the concept of proletarian class-consciousness as a mechanical product of its class situation, and with the idea that the revolution itself was only the mechanical working out of fatalistically explosive economic forces which – given the sufficient 'maturity' of objective revolutionary conditions – would somehow 'automatically' lead the proletariat to victory. If events had to be delayed until the proletariat entered the decisive struggle united and clear in its aims, there would never be a revolutionary situation. On the one hand, there will always be proletarian strata who will stand passively by and watch the liberation struggle of their own class, and even cross over to the other side – the more so, the more developed the capitalism. On the other hand, the attitude of the proletariat itself, its determination and degree of class-consciousness, by no means develops with fatalistic inevitability from its economic situation.

Naturally, even the biggest and best party imaginable cannot 'make' a revolution. But the way the proletariat reacts to a given situation largely depends on the clarity and energy which the party is able to impart to its class aims. *When the revolution is an actuality, the old problem of whether or not it can be 'made' thus acquires a completely new meaning*. This changed meaning gives rise in turn to a change in the relationship between party and class, to a change in the meaning of organizational problems for party and proletariat as a whole. The old formulation of the question about 'making' the revolution is based on an inflexible, undialectical division between historical necessity and the activity of the relevant party. On this level, where 'making' the revolution means conjuring it up out of nothing, it must be totally rejected. But the activity of the party in a revolutionary period means something fundamentally different. If the basic character of the times is revolutionary, an acutely revolutionary situation can break out at any moment. The actual time and circumstance are hardly ever exactly determinable. But the tendencies which lead towards it and the principal lines of the correct course of action to be taken when it begins are thereby all the more determinable. The party's activity is based on this historical understanding. *The party must prepare the revolution.* In other words, it must on the one hand try to *accelerate* the maturing of these revolutionary tendencies by its actions (through its influence on the proletariat and other oppressed groups). On the other hand, it must prepare the proletariat for the ideological, tactical, material and organizational tasks that necessarily arise in an acutely revolutionary situation.

This puts the internal problems of party organization in a new perspective as well. Both the old idea – held by Kautsky among others – that organization was the *precondition* of revolutionary action, and that of Rosa Luxemburg that it is a *product* of the revolutionary mass movement, appear one-sided and undialectical. Because it is the party's function to prepare the revolution, it is – simultaneously and equally – both *producer* and *product*, both precondition *and* result of the revolutionary mass movement. For the party's conscious activity is based on clear recognition of the objective inevitability of the economic process; its strict organizational exclusiveness is in constant fruitful interaction with the instinctive struggles and sufferings of the masses. Rosa Luxemburg sometimes came near an appreciation of this element of interaction, but she ignored the *conscious and active element* in it. That is why she was incapable of understanding the vital point of the Leninist party concept – the party's preparatory role – and why she was bound grossly to misinterpret all the organizational principles which followed from it.

The revolutionary situation itself can naturally not be a product of party activity. The party's role is to foresee the trajectory of the objective economic forces and to forecast what the appropriate actions of the working class must be in the situation so created. In keeping with this foresight, it must do as much as possible to prepare the proletarian masses intellectually, materially, and organizationally both for what lies ahead and how their interests relate to it. However, the actual events themselves and the situations which subsequently arise from them are a result of the economic forces of capitalist production, working themselves out blindly and according to their own natural laws – though not, even then, with mechanistic fatality. For the example of the economic decay of Russian agrarian feudalism has already shown us how the process of this decay may in itself be an inevitable result of capitalist development. But its effects in class terms – the new class alignments that arise from it – by no means either depend simply on or are therefore determinable only from this development in isolation. They are determined by their environment; in the last analysis, by the destiny of the whole society whose parts constitute this development. But within this totality, both spontaneous-explosive and consciously-led class actions play a decisive role. Moreover, the more disturbed a society is, the more completely its 'normal' structure has ceased to function, the more shaken its socio-economic balance – in other words, the more revolutionary the situation – the more decisive their role will be. This means that the total development of society in the era of capitalism by no means follows a simple, straight line. More often situations arise out of a combination of forces within society as a whole, in which a specific tendency can work itself through – provided the situation is correctly recognized and correspondingly evaluated. But if this chance is missed, if the right consequences are not drawn, the development of economic forces which appear to be set on a particular course by no means continues as irrevocably on it but very often changes to its exact opposite. (Imagine the situation in Russia if the Bolsheviks had not seized power in 1917 and completed the agrarian revolution. Under a capitalist regime, counter-revolutionary but modern compared with pre-revolutionary Tsarism, a 'Prussian' solution of the agrarian question would not have been wholly inconceivable.)

Only knowledge of the historical context in which the proletarian party has to act can give a real understanding of the problem of party organization, which depends on the immense, world-historical tasks which the period of declining capitalism places before the proletariat – the immense, world-historical responsibility these tasks lay on the shoulders of its conscious leaders. Because the party, on the basis of its knowledge of society in its totality, represents the interests of the whole proletariat (and in doing so mediates the interests of all the oppressed – the future of mankind), it must unite within it all the contradictions in which the tasks that arise from the very heart of this social totality are expressed. We have already emphasized that the strictest selection of party members according to clarity of class-consciousness and unconditional devotion to the cause of the revolution must be combined with their equal ability to merge themselves totally in the lives of the struggling and suffering masses. All efforts to fulfil the first of these demands without its corollary are bound, even where groups of good revolutionaries are concerned, to be paralysed by sectarianism. (This is the basis of the struggle Lenin led against 'the Left', from Otzovism[3] to the KAP[4] and beyond.) For the stringency of the demands made on party members is only a way of making clear to the whole proletariat (and all strata exploited by capitalism) where their true interests lie, and of making them conscious of the true basis of their hitherto unconscious actions, vague ideology and confused feelings.

But the masses can only learn through action; they can only become aware of their interests through struggle – a struggle whose socio-economic basis is constantly changing and in which *the conditions and the weapons therefore also constantly change*. The vanguard party of the proletariat can only fulfil its destiny in this conflict if it is *always a step in front* of the struggling masses, to show them the way. But only *one* step in front so that it always remains leader of *their* struggle. Its theoretical clarity is therefore only valuable if it does not stop at a general – merely theoretical – level, but always culminates in the concrete analysis of a concrete situation; in other words, if its theoretical correctness always only expresses the sense of the concrete situation. The party therefore must, on the one hand, have sufficient theoretical clarity and firmness to stay on the right course despite all the hesitations of the masses, even at the risk of temporary isolation. On the other hand, it must be so flexible and capable of learning from them that it can single out from every manifestation of the masses, however confused, the revolutionary possibilities of which they have themselves remained unconscious.

This degree of adjustment to the life of the masses *is impossible without the strictest party discipline*. If the party is not capable of immediately adjusting its interpretation to the ever-changing situation, it lags behind, follows instead of leads, loses contact with the masses and disintegrates. Party organization must therefore be of the utmost severity and rigour in order to put its ability to adjust into practice immediately, if necessary. At the same time, however, this means that the demand for flexibility must also be continuously applied to the party organization itself. A particular form of organization, useful in particular circumstances for particular purposes, can be an actual hindrance when the conditions of struggle change.

For it is of the essence of history always to create the *new*, which cannot be forecast by any infallible theory. It is through struggle that the new element must be recognized and consciously brought to light from its first embryonic appearance. In no sense is it the party's role to impose any kind of abstract, cleverly devised tactics upon the masses. On the contrary, it must continuously *learn* from their struggle and their conduct of it. But it must remain active while it learns, preparing the next revolutionary undertaking. It must unite the spontaneous discoveries of the masses, which originate in their correct class instincts, with the totality of the revolutionary struggle, and bring them to consciousness. In Marx's words, it must explain their own actions to the masses, so as not only to preserve the continuity of the proletariat's revolutionary experiences, but also consciously and actively to contribute to their further development. The party organization must adapt itself to become an instrument both of this totality and of the actions which result from it. If it fails to do this it will sabotage developments which it has not understood and therefore not mastered. Therefore, *all dogmatism in theory and all sclerosis in organization are disastrous for the party*. For as Lenin said: 'Every new form of struggle which brings new perils and sacrifices inevitably "disorganizes" an organization ill-prepared for the new form of struggle. It is the party's task to pursue its necessary path openly and consciously – above all in relation to itself – so that it may transform itself before the danger of disorganization becomes acute, and by this transformation promote the transformation and advance of the masses.'

For tactics and organization are only two sides of an indivisible whole. *Real results can only be achieved in both at once*. For this to happen, the party must be consistent and flexible in adhering stubbornly to its principles and simultaneously holding itself open to each new daily development. Neither tactically nor organizationally can anything be either good or bad in itself. Only its relation to the whole, to the fate of the proletarian revolution, makes a thought, a policy decision, etc., right or wrong. That is why, for example, after the First Russian Revolution of 1905, Lenin fought relentlessly both against those who wanted to abandon an allegedly useless and sectarian illegality and those who devoted themselves unreservedly to it, rejecting the possibilities available to them under legality; why he had the same angry contempt both for surrender to parliamentarianism and for principled anti-parliamentarianism.

Lenin not only never became a political utopian; he also never had any illusions about the human material around him. 'We want,' he said in the first heroic period of the victorious proletarian revolution, 'to build socialism with people who, reared as they were under capitalism, have been distorted and corrupted, but also steeled for battle, by it.' The immense demands which Lenin's concept of party organization made upon professional revolutionaries were not in themselves utopian, nor did they naturally have much connexion with the superficiality of ordinary life. They were not concerned with the immediate facts; they went beyond mere empiricism. Lenin's concept of organization is in itself dialectical: it is both a product of and a conscious contributor to, historical development in so far as it, too, *is simultaneously product and producer of itself.* Men themselves build a party. A high degree of class-consciousness and devotion is required in order to want and to be capable of working in a party organization at all. However, only by being so organized and by working through a party can men become real professional revolutionaries. The individual Jacobin who joins the revolutionary class can shape and clarify its actions through his determination, militancy, knowledge, and enthusiasm. But the social existence of the class and its resulting class-consciousness must always determine the content and trajectory of his actions, which are not undertaken by him on behalf of the class but are the culmination of class activity itself.

The party called upon to lead the proletarian revolution is not born ready-made into its leading role: it, too, *is* not but *is becoming*. And the process of fruitful interaction between party and class repeats itself – albeit differently – in the relationship between the party and its members. For as Marx said in his theses on Feuerbach: 'The materialist doctrine concerning the changing of circumstances and education forgets that circumstances are changed by men and that the educator must himself be educated.' The Leninist party concept represents the most radical break with the mechanistic and fatalistic vulgarization of Marxism. It is, on the contrary, the practical realization both of its genuine essence and its deepest intent: 'The philosophers have only *interpreted* the world in different ways; the point, however, is to change it.'

4. Imperialism:
World War and Civil War

But have we entered the period of decisive revolutionary struggles? Has the moment already come when the proletariat, on pain of its own destruction, is forced to take up its task of changing the world? For it is clear that even the most mature proletarian ideology or organization is unable to bring about such a crisis unless this maturity and militancy is a result of the objective socio-economic world situation itself pressing for a solution. Nor can a single isolated event, regardless of whether it is a victory or a defeat, possibly decide this. It is even impossible to say whether such an event is either a victory or a defeat; only in relation to the totality of socio-historic development can it be termed either one or the other in a world-historical sense.

This is why the dispute – which broke out during the actual course of the First Revolution (1905) and reached its climax after its defeat – in Russian Social Democrat circles (then both Menshevik and Bolshevik) as to whether the correct parallel was with the situation in 1847 (*before* the decisive revolution) or 1848 (*after its defeat*) inevitably extends beyond the Russian context in the narrow sense. It can only be resolved when the question of the fundamental character of our time is resolved. The more limited, specifically Russian, question as to whether the 1905 Revolution was bourgeois or proletarian and whether the proletarian revolutionary position taken by the workers was correct or 'mistaken' can only be answered in this context. To be sure, the very fact that the question was raised with such vigour indicates where the answer lies. For outside Russia, too, the division between Left and Right within the labour movement increasingly begins to take the form of a debate about the general character of the times: a debate about whether specific, increasingly manifest, economic phenomena (concentration of capital, growing importance of big banks, colonization) mark only quantitative changes within 'normal' capitalist development, or whether it is possible to deduce from them the approach of a new capitalist epoch – that of imperialism; whether the increasingly frequent wars (Boer War, Spanish-American War, Russo-Japanese War), following as they do a relatively peaceful period, are to be regarded as 'accidents' or 'episodes', or whether they are to be seen as the first signs of a period of even greater confrontations; and finally – if all this indicates that the development of capitalism has entered a new phase – whether the old forms of proletarian struggle are sufficient to express the proletariat's class interests under the new conditions. Are, therefore, those new forms of proletarian class struggle which developed before and during the First Russian Revolution (the mass strike, armed uprising), phenomena of only local particular significance – 'mistakes' even, or 'aberrations' – or should they be regarded as the first spontaneous attempts by the masses, on the basis of their correct class instincts, to adjust their actions to the world situation?

Lenin's practical answer to the interconnected complex of these questions is well known. It found its clearest expression immediately after the defeat of the First Revolution, at a time when Menshevik lamentations about the mistakes of the Russian workers in 'going too far' had not yet died away. Lenin then took up the struggle at the Stuttgart Congress to make the Second International adopt a clear and strong stand against the directly threatening danger of an imperialist world war, and to pose the question: *what could be done to prevent such a war?*

The Lenin-Luxemburg amendment was accepted in Stuttgart and later ratified at the Copenhagen and Basle

Congresses. The danger of an approaching world war and the necessity for the proletariat to conduct a revolutionary struggle against it were thus officially admitted by the Second International. So Lenin apparently by no means stood alone on this issue. Neither was he alone in recognizing imperialism economically as a new phase of capitalism. The whole Left and even parts of the Centre and the Right of the Second International recognized the economic roots of imperialism. Hilferding tried to provide a new economic theory for the new phenomena, and Rosa Luxemburg went even further and succeeded in representing the entire economic system of imperialism as an inevitable consequence of the process of the reproduction of capital – incorporating imperialism organically into the theory of historical materialism, thus giving 'the theory of capitalist collapse' a concrete economic foundation. Yet it was no mere chance that, in August 1914 and for a long time thereafter, Lenin stood quite alone in his attitude to the world war. Much less can it be explained psychologically or morally, by arguing that perhaps many others who had earlier made an equally 'correct' assessment of imperialism had now become hesitant out of 'cowardice'. On the contrary: *the different attitudes of the various socialist currents in 1914 were the direct, logical consequences of their theoretical, tactical, and other positions up till then.*

In an apparent paradox, the Leninist concept of imperialism is both a significant theoretical achievement, and contains as economic theory little that is really new. It is partly based on Hilferding and, purely as economics, by no means bears comparison in depth and sweep with Rosa Luxemburg's admirable extension of Marx's theory of capitalist reproduction. Lenin's superiority – and this is an unparalleled theoretical achievement – consists in *his concrete articulation of the economic theory of imperialism with every political problem of the present epoch*, thereby making the economics of the new phase a guide-line for all concrete action in the resultant decisive conjuncture. That is why, for example, during the war he rejected certain Polish Communist ultra-left views as 'imperialist economism',[5] and why his fight against Kautsky's concept of 'Ultra-Imperialism'[6] – which expressed hopes for a peaceful international trust towards which world war was an 'accidental' and not even 'correct' path – culminates in the charge that Kautsky separates the economics of imperialism from its politics. It is true that the theory of imperialism elaborated by Rosa Luxemburg (also by Pannekoek[7] and others on the left) does not suffer from economism in the narrow, real sense of the word. All of them – especially Rosa Luxemburg – stress just that moment in the economics of imperialism when it is necessarily transformed into politics. Yet this connexion is not made concrete. Rosa Luxemburg demonstrates incomparably how, as a result of the process of accumulation, the transition to imperialism as the epoch of struggle for colonial outlets, raw materials and export of capital, has become unavoidable; how this epoch – the last stage of capitalism – is bound to be one of world wars. In doing so, however, she establishes merely the theory of the epoch *as a whole* – the *overall* theory of modern imperialism. She, too, is unable to make the transition from this theory to the concrete demands of the day: it is impossible to establish an inevitable continuity linking *The Accumulation of Capital* with the concrete passages of the *Juniusbrochüre*.[8] She does not concretize her theoretically correct assessment of the epoch as a whole into a clear recognition of those particular moving forces which it is the practical task of Marxist theory to evaluate and to exploit in a revolutionary way.

However, Lenin's superiority here cannot by any means be explained away by cliché references to 'political genius' or 'practical ingenuity'. It is far more *a purely theoretical superiority in assessing the total process.* For Lenin did not make a single practical decision in his whole life which was not the rational and logical outcome of his theoretical standpoint. That the fundamental axiom of this standpoint is the demand for the concrete analysis of the concrete situation removes the issue to one of *realpolitik* only for those who do not think dialectically. *For Marxists the concrete analysis of the concrete situation* is not the opposite of 'pure' theory; on the contrary, it is *the culmination of all genuine theory*, its consummation, the point where it therefore breaks into practice.

The basis of this theoretical superiority is that, of all Marx's followers, Lenin's vision was least distorted by the fetishist categories of his capitalist environment. For the decisive superiority of Marxist economics over all its predecessors and successors lies in its methodological ability to interpret even the most complex questions which, to all appearances, have to be treated in the most purely economic (therefore, most purely fetishist) categories, in such a way that behind these categories the evolution of those classes whose social existence they express becomes visible. (Compare, for example, the difference between Marx's concept of constant and variable capital, and the classical division between fixed and circulating capital. Only through this differentiation was the class structure of bourgeois society clearly revealed. The Marxist interpretation of surplus value already exposed the class stratification between bourgeoisie and proletariat. The additional concept of constant capital showed how this relationship was dynamically connected with the development of society as a whole, and at the same time exposed the struggle of the different capitalist interest groups for the division of surplus value.)

Lenin's theory of imperialism, unlike Rosa Luxemburg's, is less a theory of its necessary economic generation and limitations than the theory of the concrete class forces which, unleashed by imperialism, are at work within it: *the theory of the concrete world situation created by imperialism.* When Lenin studies the essence of monopoly capitalism, what primarily interests him is this concrete world situation and the class alignments created by it: how the world has been *de facto* divided up by the colonial powers; how the concentration of capital effects changes within the class stratification of bourgeoisie and proletariat (appearance of purely parasitic *rentiers*, labour aristocracy); and above all, how, because of its different momentum in different countries, the development of monopoly capitalism itself invalidates the temporary peaceful distribution of 'spheres of interest' and other compromises, and drives it to conflicts which can only be resolved by force – in other words, by war.

Because the essence of imperialism is monopoly capitalism, and its war is the inevitable development and expression of this trend to still greater concentration and to absolute monopoly, the relation of social groups within capitalist society to war emerges very clearly. The idea – *à la* Kautsky – that sections of the bourgeoisie 'not directly interested' in imperialism, who are even 'defrauded' by it, can be mobilized against it, shows itself to be naïve self-deception. Monopoly development sweeps the whole of the bourgeoisie along with it. What is more, it finds support not only in the inherently vacillating petty bourgeoisie, but even (albeit temporarily) among sections of the proletariat. However, the faint-hearted are wrong in thinking that, because of its unqualified rejection of imperialism, the revolutionary proletariat becomes socially isolated. The development of capitalist society is always inconsistent, always contradictory. Monopoly capitalism creates a real world economy for the first time in history. It follows that its war, imperialist war, is the first world war in the strictest sense of the term. This means, above all, that for the first time in history the nations oppressed and exploited by capitalism no longer fight isolated wars against their oppressors but are swept up as a whole into the maelstrom of the world war. In its developed form capitalist exploitation does not just criminally exploit the colonial peoples as it did at its outset; *it simultaneously transforms their whole social structure and draws them into the capitalist system*. Naturally, this only happens in the course of the search for greater exploitation (export of capital, etc.); it results in the establishment of the basis of an indigenous bourgeois development in the colonies – naturally looked upon with ill-favour by imperialism – of which the inevitable ideological consequence is *the onset of the struggle for national independence.* This whole process is intensified still further because imperialist war mobilizes all available human resources in the imperialist countries while it simultaneously drags the colonial people actively into the fighting and speeds up the development of their industries – in other words, accelerates the process of national struggle both economically and ideologically.

But the position of the colonial peoples is only an extreme form of the relationship between monopoly capitalism and those normally exploited by it. The historical transition from one epoch to another is never mechanical: a particular mode of production does not develop and play a historic role only when the mode superseded by it has already everywhere completed the social transformations appropriate to it. The modes of production and the corresponding social forms and class stratifications which succeed and supersede one another tend in fact to appear in history much more as intersecting and opposing forces. In this way, developments which seem to be invariable in the abstract (for instance, the transition from feudalism to capitalism) acquire an entirely different relationship to the socio-historic whole because of the totally changed historical milieu in which they take place, and accordingly take on a completely new function and significance in their own right.

Emergent capitalism appeared as an important factor in the formation of European nations. After profound revolutionary struggles, it transformed the chaos of small medieval feudal governments into great nations in the most capitalistically developed part of Europe. The movements for the unity of Germany and Italy were the last of these objectively revolutionary struggles. But if capitalism has developed into imperialist monopoly capitalism in these new states, if it even began to take on such forms in some of the more backward countries (Russia, Japan), this does not mean that its significance as a nation-building factor ceased for the whole of the rest of the world. On the contrary, *continuing capitalist development created national movements among all the hitherto 'unhistoric' nations of Europe.* The difference is that their 'struggles for national liberation' are now no longer merely struggles against their own feudalism and feudal absolutism – that is to say only implicitly progressive – for *they are forced into the context of imperialist rivalry between the world powers.* Their historical significance, their evaluation, therefore depends on what concrete part they play in this concrete whole.

Marx had already clearly recognized the significance of this. In his time it was admittedly mainly an English problem: the problem of England's relation to Ireland. And Marx stressed with the greatest force that, 'questions of international justice apart, it is a precondition of the emancipation of the English working class to transform the present enforced union – in other words, slavery of – Ireland, if possible into an equal and free alliance and, if necessary, into total separation'. For he had clearly seen that the exploitation of Ireland was, on the one hand, an important bastion of English capitalism which was already – at that time uniquely – monopolist in character, and on the other, that the ambiguous attitude of the English working class to this issue divided the oppressed, provoked a struggle of exploited against exploited instead of their united struggle against their common exploiters, and that therefore only the struggle for the national liberation of Ireland could create a really effective front in the English proletariat's struggle against its own bourgeoisie.

This conception of Marx's remained ineffective not only within the contemporary English labour movement; it also remained dead in both the theory and the practice of the Second International. Here too it was left to Lenin to instil new life into the theory – a more active, more concrete life than even Marx had given it himself. For from being simply a universal fact it had become a topical issue and, in Lenin, is found correspondingly no longer as theory but purely as practice. For it must be obvious to everyone in this context that the problem which here confronts us in all its magnitude – the rebellion of all the oppressed, not only the workers, on a universal scale – *is the same problem that Lenin had always persistently proclaimed to be at the core of the Russian agrarian question – against the Narodniks, Legal Marxists, and Economists*. The crucial point at issue is what Rosa Luxemburg called capitalism's 'external' market, regardless of whether it lies inside or outside the national frontiers. On the one hand, expanding capitalism cannot exist without it; on the other, its social function in relation to this market consists in breaking down its original structure, in making it capitalist, in transforming it into a capitalist 'internal' market, thus at the same time stimulating in turn its own independent tendencies. So here too the relationship is dialectical. But Rosa Luxemburg did not find the path from this correct and broad historical perspective to the concrete solutions of the concrete questions raised by the world war. It remained for her an historical perspective – an accurate and broadly conceived characterization of the whole epoch, but of it only as a whole. It was left to Lenin to make the step from theory to practice; a step which is simultaneously – and this should never be forgotten – *a theoretical advance*. For it is a step from the abstract to the concrete.

This transition to the concrete from the abstract correct assessment of actual historical reality, on the basis of the proven general revolutionary character of the whole imperialist epoch, culminates in the question of the specific character of the revolution. One of Marx's greatest theoretical achievements was to distinguish clearly between bourgeois and proletarian revolution. This distinction was of the utmost practical and tactical importance in view of the immature self-delusions of his contemporaries, for it offered the only methodological instrument for recognizing the genuinely proletarian revolutionary elements within the general revolutionary movements of the time. *In vulgar Marxism this distinction is, however, paralysed into a mechanistic separation.* For opportunists, the practical consequence of this separation is the schematic generalization of the empirically correct observation that practically every modern revolution begins as a bourgeois revolution, however many proletarian actions or demands may arise within it. The opportunists conclude from this that the revolution is only a bourgeois one and that it is the task of the proletariat to support *this* revolution. From this separation of the bourgeois from the proletarian revolution follows *the renunciation by the proletariat of its own revolutionary class aims.*

But the radical left-wing analysis, which easily sees through the mechanistic fallacy of this theory and is conscious of the age's proletarian revolutionary character, is in turn subject to an equally dangerous mechanistic interpretation. Knowing that, in the age of imperialism, the universal revolutionary role of the bourgeoisie is at an end, it concludes – also on the basis of the mechanistic separation of the bourgeois and the proletarian revolution – that *we have now finally entered the age of the purely proletarian revolution.* The dangerous practical consequence of this attitude is that all those tendencies towards decay and fermentation which necessarily arise under imperialism (the agrarian, colonial and national questions, etc.), *which are objectively revolutionary within the context of the proletarian revolution*, are overlooked, or even despised and rebuffed. These theoreticians of the purely proletarian revolution voluntarily reject the most effective and most important of their allies; they ignore precisely that revolutionary environment which makes the proletarian revolution concretely promising, hoping and thinking in a vacuum that they are preparing a 'purely' proletarian revolution. 'Whoever expects a "pure" social revolution,' said Lenin, 'will *never* live to see one. Such a person pays lip-service to revolution without understanding what revolution is.'

For the real revolution is the dialectical transformation of the bourgeois revolution into the proletarian revolution. The undeniable historical fact that the class which led or was the beneficiary of the great bourgeois revolutions of the past becomes objectively counter-revolutionary does not mean that those objective problems on which its revolution turned have found their social solutions – that those strata of society who were vitally interested in the revolutionary solution of these problems have been satisfied. On the contrary, the bourgeoisie's recourse to counter-revolution indicates not only its hostility towards the proletariat, but at the same time the renunciation of its own revolutionary traditions. *It abandons the inheritance of its revolutionary past to the proletariat.* From now on the proletariat is the only class capable of taking the bourgeois revolution to its logical conclusion. In other words, the remaining relevant demands of the bourgeois revolution can only be realized within the framework of the proletarian revolution, and the consistent realization of these demands necessarily leads to a proletarian revolution. Thus, the proletarian revolution now means at one and the same time the realization and the supersession of the bourgeois revolution.

The correct appreciation of this situation opens up an immense perspective for the chances and possibilites of the proletarian revolution. At the same time, however, it makes heavy demands on the revolutionary proletariat and its leading party. For to achieve this dialectical transition the proletariat must not only have the right insight into the right context, but must in practice overcome all its own petty-bourgeois tendencies and habits of thought (for instance, national prejudice), which have hitherto prevented such insight. *Overcoming its own limitations, the proletariat must rise to the leadership of all the oppressed.* The oppressed nations' struggle for national independence is an undertaking of the greatest revolutionary self-education, both for the proletariat of the oppressing nation, which overcomes its own nationalism by fighting for the full national independence of another people, and for the proletariat of the oppressed nation, which in its turn transcends its own nationalism by raising the corresponding slogan of federalism – of international proletarian solidarity. For as Lenin says, 'The proletariat struggles for socialism and against its own weaknesses.' The struggle for the revolution, the exploitation of objective opportunities in the world situation, and the internal struggle for the maturity of its own revolutionary class-consciousness are inseparable elements of one and the same dialectical process.

Imperialist war, therefore, creates allies for the proletariat everywhere *provided it takes up a revolutionary struggle against the bourgeoisie*. But if it remains unconscious of its position and the tasks confronting it, the war forces the proletariat to disastrous self-emasculation in the wake of the bourgeoisie. Imperialist war creates a world situation in which the proletariat can become the real leader of all the oppressed and exploited, and in which its struggle for liberation can become the signal and signpost for the liberation of all those under the capitalist yoke. At the same time, however, it creates a world situation in which millions and millions of proletarians must murder each other with the most refined cruelty in order to strengthen and extend the monopoly of their exploiters. Which of these two fates is to be that of the proletariat *depends upon its insight into its own historical situation – upon its class-consciousness*. For 'men make their own history', although 'not in circumstances chosen by themselves but in circumstances directly encountered, given and transmitted from the past'. So the choice is not *whether* the proletariat will or will not struggle, but *in whose interest* it should struggle: its own or that of the bourgeoisie. The question history places before the proletariat is *not to choose between war and peace, but between imperialist war and war against this war: civil war*.

The necessity of civil war in the proletariat's defence against imperialist war originates, like all proletarian forms of struggle, in the conditions of struggle imposed upon it by the development of capitalist production in bourgeois society. The activity and correct theoretical foresight of the party only endows the proletariat with a power of resistance or attack which, because of the existing class alignments, it already objectively possesses but is unable to raise to the level of the possibilities before it, owing to theoretical or organizational immaturity. Thus, even before the imperialist war, the mass strike appeared as the spontaneous reaction of the proletariat to the imperialist stage of capitalism, and the connexion between the two which the Right and Centre of the Second International did their best to conceal, gradually became the common theoretical property of the radical wing.

But here too Lenin was alone in realizing, as early as 1905, that the mass strike was an insufficient weapon for the decisive struggle. By evaluating the Moscow Uprising, despite its defeat, as a vital phase in the struggle, and by attempting to establish its concrete elements, in contrast to Plekhanov who thought that 'there should have been no resort to arms', *Lenin already laid down in theory the necessary tactics of the proletariat in the world war.* For the imperialist stage of capitalism, particularly its climax in world war, shows that capitalism has entered the crucial phase when its very existence is in the balance. With the correct instinct of an habitual ruling class, conscious that the real social basis of its authority narrows as the extent of its rule grows and its power apparatus increases, the bourgeoisie makes the most energetic efforts both to broaden this basis (alignment of the middle class behind it, corruption of the labour aristocracy, etc.), and to defeat its chief enemies decisively before they have organized for real resistance. Thus, it is everywhere the bourgeoisie which abolishes 'peaceful' means of conducting the class struggle, on the temporary, if highly problematic functioning of which the whole theory of Revisionism was based, and which prefers 'more energetic' weapons (one need only consider the situation in America[9]). The bourgeoisie increasingly succeeds in seizing control of the state apparatus, in identifying itself so completely with it that even demands of the working class which appear only to be economic are increasingly blocked by it. Thus, if only to prevent the deterioration of their economic condition and the loss of vanatage points already gained, the workers are compelled to take up the struggle against state power (in other words, though unconsciously, the struggle for state power). This forces the proletariat into using the tactics of the mass strike, in the course of which, for fear of revolution, the opportunists are always intent on giving up positions already gained rather than on drawing the revolutionary conclusions from the situation. But the mass strike is by its very nature an objectively revolutionary weapon. Every mass strike creates a revolutionary situation in which the bourgeoisie, supported by its state apparatus, takes the necessary steps against it wherever possible. The proletariat is powerless against such measures. The weapon of the mass strike is also bound to fail against them if the proletariat, faced with the aims of the bourgeoisie, does not also take to arms. This means that it must try and equip itself, disorganize the army of the bourgeoisie – which of course consists mainly of workers and peasants – and turn the weapons of the bourgeoisie against the bourgeoisie. (The 1905 Revolution offered many examples of correct class instinct, but only of instinct, in this respect.)

Imperialist war means the sharpening of this situation to its utmost extremity. The bourgeoisie confronts the proletariat with the choice: either to kill its class comrades in other countries for the monopolistic interests of the bourgeoisie and die for these interests, or to overthrow the rule of the bourgeoisie by force. All other methods of struggle against this wholesale assault are powerless; all without exception would smash themselves against the military apparatus of the imperialist states. If the proletariat wants to escape this ultimate onslaught, it must therefore itself take up arms against this apparatus, undermine it from within, turn the weapons the bourgeoisie was forced to give to the people against the bourgeoisie itself, and use them to destroy imperialism.

So here too there is nothing theoretically in the least unprecedented. On the contrary, the core of the situation lies in the class relationship between bourgeoisie and proletariat. War is, as Clausewitz defined it, only the continuation of politics; but it is so *in all respects*. In other words, it is not only in foreign affairs that war is merely the ultimate and most active culmination of a policy which a country has hitherto followed 'peacefully'. For the internal class relations of a country as well (and of the whole world), it only marks the intensification and ultimate climax of those tendencies which were already at work within society in 'peacetime'. Therefore war by no means creates a totally new situation, either for a country or for a class within a nation. What is new about it is merely that the unprecedented quantitative intensification of all problems involves a qualitative change and for this – and only for this – reason creates a new situation.

Socio-economically war is therefore only a stage in the imperialist development of capitalism. It is thus also necessarily only a stage in the class struggle of the proletariat against the bourgeoisie. The Leninist theory of imperialism is significant because Lenin alone established this relationship between world war and historical development as a whole with theoretical consistency, and clearly proved it on the basis of concrete problems posed by the war. But because historical materialism is the theory of proletarian class struggle, the establishment of this relationship would have remained incomplete *if the theory of imperialism had not simultaneously become a theory of the different currents within the working-class movement in the age of imperialism*. It was not only a question of seeing clearly what action was in the interest of the proletariat in the new world situation created by the war, but also of theoretically demonstrating the basis of the other 'proletarian' attitudes to imperialism and its war – what social modifications within the proletariat gave these theories sufficient following for them to become political currents.

Above all it was necessary to show that these different currents did exist as such; to show that the Social Democrats' attitude to the war was not the result of a momentary aberration or of cowardice, but was a necessary consequence of their immediate past; *that it was to be understood within the context of the history of the labour movement* and related to previous 'differences of opinion' within the Social Democratic Party (Revisionism, etc.). Yet, although this idea should come naturally to Marxist methodology (see the treatment of the contemporary currents in *The Communist Manifesto*), it only penetrated even the revolutionary wing of the movement with difficulty. Even the Rosa Luxemburg-Franz Mehring *Internationale* group[10] were incapable of thinking it through and applying it consistently. It is however clear that any condemnation of opportunism and its attitude towards the war which fails to interpret it as an historically recognizable current in the labour movement, and which does not see its present existence as the organically developed fruit of its past, neither attains the level of a really principled Marxist discussion, nor draws from the condemnation the practical-concrete, tactical-organizational conclusions necessary when the time for action comes.

For Lenin, and again only for Lenin, it was clear from the onset of the world war that the attitude of Scheidemann, Plekhanov or Vandervelde towards it was merely *the consistent application of the principles of Revisionism in the new situation*.

What, in short, constitutes the essence of Revisionism? First, that it tries to overcome the 'one-sidedness' of historical materialism – in other words, the interpretation of *all* socio-historic phenomena *exclusively* from the class standpoint of the proletariat. Revisionism takes the interests of 'society as a whole' as its standpoint. But because such a collective interest has no concrete existence – for what can appear as such an interest is only the temporary result of the interaction of different class forces in mutual struggle – *the Revisionist takes an ever-changing product of the historical process as a fixed theoretical starting-point*. Thus he stands things theoretically on their head as well. In practice he is always essentially a figure of compromise: necessarily so, because of this theoretical starting-point. Revisionism is always eclectic. Even at a theoretical level it tries to blur and blunt class differences, and to make a unity of classes – an upside-down unity which only exists in its own head – the criterion for judging events.

The Revisionist thus in the second place condemns *the dialectic*. For the dialectic is no more than the conceptual expression of the fact that the development of society is in reality contradictory, and that these contradictions (class contradictions, the antagonistic character of their economic existence, etc.) are the basis and kernel of all events; for in so far as society is built on class divisions, the idea of its 'unity' can only be abstract – a perpetually transitory result of the interaction of these contradictions. But because the dialectic as a method is only the theoretical formulation of the fact that society develops by a process of contradictions, in a state of transformation from one contradiction to another, in other words *in a revolutionary fashion*, theoretical rejection of it necessarily means an essential break with the whole revolutionary standpoint.

Because the Revisionists thus, thirdly, refuse to recognize the real existence of the dialectic, with its contradictory and thereby permanently *creative* movement, their thought always lacks historical, concrete and creative dimensions. Their reality is subject to schematic and mechanistic 'eternal, fixed laws' which continuously – according to their different properties – produce the *same* phenomena, to which mankind is fatally subjected as it is to natural laws. For Revisionists it is therefore enough to know these laws once and for all in order to know what the fate of the proletariat will be. They consider it unscientific to suppose that there can be new situations not covered by these laws, or situations whose outcome depends on the will of the proletariat. (Over-emphasis on great men or ethics is only the inevitable obverse of this attitude.)

Fourth, however, these laws are seen as *the laws of capitalist development*, and the emphasis Revisionists put on their supra-historical, timeless validity means that they regard society as *the reality* which cannot essentially be changed just as much as the bourgeoisie. They no longer regard bourgeois society as historically created and therefore destined to historical decline. Nor do they regard knowledge as a means of recognizing this period of decline and of working for its acceleration, but – at best – as a means of improving the condition of the proletariat *within bourgeois society*. For Revisionism, all thought which points in a practical way beyond the horizons of bourgeois society is illusory and utopian.

Revisionism is therefore – fifth – tied to *realpolitik. It always sacrifices the genuine interests of the class as a whole*, the consistent representation of which is precisely what it calls utopian, *so as to represent the immediate interests of specific groups.*

These few remarks alone are enough to make it clear that Revisionism could only become a real current within the labour movement because the new development of capitalism made it temporarily possible for certain groups among the workers to obtain economic advantages from it, and because the organizational structure of the working-class parties ensured these groups and their intellectual representatives greater influence than the instinctively if confusedly revolutionary broad mass of the proletariat.

The common character of all opportunist currents is that they never regard events from the class standpoint of the proletariat and therefore fall victim to an unhistorical, undialectical, and eclectic *realpolitik*. This is what unites their different interpretations of the war and reveals these to be without exception the inevitable consequence of their previous opportunism. The unconditional support which the Right offers the imperialist forces of its 'own' country develops organically from the view, however qualified at the outset, which sees in the bourgeoisie the leading class in the future development of history and assigns the proletariat the task of supporting its 'progressive role'. And if Kautsky terms the International an instrument of peace and hence unsuitable for war, how does he differ from the Menshevik Cheravanin, who lamented after the First Russian Revolution: 'It is indeed hard to find a place for sensible Menshevik tactics in the midst of revolutionary action, when revolutionary aims are so near their fulfilment.'?

Opportunism differs *according to the strata of the bourgeoisie with which it tries to unite* and in whose support it attempts to enlist the proletariat. For the Right, this can be with heavy industry and finance capital. In this case imperialism will be unconditionally accepted as necessary. The proletariat is supposed to find the fulfilment of its own interests actually *in* imperialist war, in grandeur, in its 'own' nation's victory. Or union can be sought with those bourgeois who feel that they have been pushed into a position of secondary importance, although forced to collaborate with imperialism; necessarily supporters of it in practice, they yet complain about its pressure and 'wish' events would take a different turn, and therefore long for peace, free trade, and a return to 'normal' conditions as soon as possible. Such elements are naturally never in a position to emerge as active opponents of imperialism; indeed they merely conduct an unsuccessful campaign for their share of its booty (some sections of light industry and the petty bourgeoisie come into this category). To them imperialism is an 'accident'. They try to work towards a pacifist solution and to blunt its contradictions. The proletariat too – whom the Centre of the Social Democratic Party wants to make the adherents of this stratum – is not supposed to fight actively against the war (although not to do so means in practice taking a part in it), but merely to preach the necessity of a 'just' peace, etc.

The International is the organizational expression of the common interests of the whole world proletariat. The moment it is accepted in theory that workers can fight workers in the service of the bourgeoisie, the International in practice ceases to exist. The moment it can no longer be concealed that this bloody struggle of worker against worker for the sake of the rival imperialist powers is an inevitable consequence of the past attitude of decisive sections within the International, there can be no more talk of rebuilding it, of its being brought back on to the right path, or of its restoration. The recognition of opportunism as a current within the International means *that opportunism is the class enemy of the proletariat within its own camp.* The removal of opportunists from the labour movement is therefore the first, essential prerequisite of the successful start of the struggle against the bourgeoisie. It is therefore of paramount importance for the preparation of the proletarian revolution to free workers intellectually and organizationally from this ruinous influence. And because this struggle is precisely the struggle of the class as a whole against the world bourgeoisie, the struggle against opportunism inevitably results in the creation of a new proletarian-revolutionary International.

The decline of the old International into the swamp of opportunism is the result of a period whose revolutionary character was not visible on the surface. Its collapse and the necessity of a new International are signs that the onset of a period of civil wars is now unavoidable. This does not by any means signify that every day from now on should be spent fighting on the barricades. But it does mean that the necessity to do so *can* arise immediately, any day; that history has placed civil war on the agenda. Accordingly, a proletarian party, let alone an International, can only survive if it clearly recognizes this necessity and is determined to prepare the proletariat for it intellectually and materially, theoretically and organizationally.

This preparation must start from an understanding of the character of the times. Only when the working class recognizes world war as the logical result of imperialist development, when it clearly sees that *civil war is the only possible resistance* to its own destruction in the service of imperialism, can the material and organizational preparation of this resistance begin. Only when this resistance is effective will the muffled stirrings of all the oppressed link up with the proletariat in the fight for its own liberation. The proletariat must therefore, first and foremost, have its own correct class-consciousness tangibly before it so that it may thereby become the leader of the true struggle for liberation – the real world revolution. The International which grows from and for this struggle, with theoretical clarity and militant strength, is thus the union of the genuinely revolutionary elements of the working class. It is simultaneously the organ and focus of the struggle of the oppressed people throughout the world for their liberation. *It is the Bolshevik Party – Lenin's concept of the party – on a world scale.* Just as the world war revealed the forces of declining capitalism and the possibilities of opposing them in the macrocosm of gigantic universal destruction, so Lenin clearly saw the possibilities of the Russian Revolution in the microcosm of nascent Russian capitalism.

5. The State as Weapon

A period's revolutionary essence is expressed most clearly when class and inter-party struggles no longer take place within the existing state order but begin to explode its barriers and point beyond them. On the one hand they appear as struggles *for* state power; on the other, the state itself is simultaneously forced *to participate* openly in them. There is not only a struggle *against* the state; the state itself is exposed as a *weapon of class struggle*, as one of the most important instruments for the maintenance of class rule.

This character of the state had always been recognized by Marx and Engels, who examined its relation to historical development and to proletarian revolution in all its aspects. They laid the theoretical foundations for a theory of the state in unmistakable terms within the framework of historical materialism. Logically enough it is precisely on this issue that opportunism deviates furthest from them. On all other issues it was possible to present (like Bernstein) the 'revision' of particular economic theories as if their basis were still – after all – consistent with the essence of Marx's method, or (like Kautsky) to give the 'orthodox' consolidated economic theory a mechanistic and fatalistic slant. But the mere raising of those problems regarded by Marx and Engels as fundamental to their theory of the state involves in itself the recognition of the actuality of the proletarian revolution. The opportunism of all the leading currents in the Second International is illustrated most clearly by the fact that none of them dealt seriously with the problem of the state. On this decisive issue there is no difference between Kautsky and Bernstein. All, without exception, simply accepted the bourgeois state. If they did criticize it, they only did so to oppose merely isolated aspects and manifestations of it harmful to the proletariat. The state was regarded exclusively from the perspective of specific day-to-day issues; its character was never examined and evaluated from that of the proletariat as a whole. The revolutionary immaturity and confusion of the left wing of the Second International is also shown in its equal incapacity to clarify the problem of the state. It went, at times, as far as dealing with the problem of revolution, of fighting *against* the state, but it was unable concretely to formulate the problem of the state itself even at a purely theoretical level, let alone point out its concrete practical consequences in historical reality.

Here again Lenin was alone in regaining the theoretical heights of Marx's conception – the clarity of the proletarian revolutionary attitude to the state. Had he done no more than this, his would have been a theoretical achievement of a high order. But, for him, this revival of Marx's theory of the state was neither a philological rediscovery of the original teaching, nor a philosophical systematization of its genuine principles. As always with Lenin, it was the extension of theory into the concrete, its concretization in everyday practice. *Lenin realized that the question of the state was now one of the struggling proletariat's immediate tasks* and represented it as such. In doing this he had already taken a step towards making it concrete (here we merely signify the importance of his even raising the question). Prior to him, the historical materialist theory of the state, brilliantly clear though it was, was only understood as a general theory – as an historical, economic or philosophical explanation of the state. Hence it was objectively possible for opportunists to obscure it. Marx and Engels derived the real evolution of the proletarian idea of the state from the concrete revolutionary events of their time (for instance, the Commune), and they were quick to point out those mistakes to which false theories of the state give rise in the course of the proletarian struggle (see *The Critique of the Gotha Programme*). Yet even their immediate followers, the outstanding socialist leaders of the time, failed to understand the *relationship* between the problem of the state and their own daily activity. The theoretical genius of Marx and Engels was needed to articulate with the minor everyday struggles what was in this context actual in only a universal sense. The proletariat itself was obviously even less in a position to make the organic connexion between this central problem and the apparently immediate problems of its own daily struggles. The problem of the state, therefore, came increasingly to be seen as merely related to 'the final goal' whose realization was to be left to the future.

Only with Lenin did this 'future' become present in the theoretical sense as well. But only if the problem of the state is recognized as immediate is it possible for the proletariat to achieve a correct approach to the capitalist state and no longer regard it as its unalterable natural environment and the only possible social order for its present existence. Only such an attitude to the bourgeois state gives the proletariat theoretical freedom towards it and makes its attitude towards it a purely tactical question. For instance, it is immediately apparent that both the tactics of legality at any price and those of a romantic illegality conceal an equal lack of theoretical freedom towards the bourgeois state, which is then not seen as a bourgeois instrument of class struggle to be reckoned with as a real power factor and *only* as such, respect for which must be reduced to a *question of mere expediency*.

But the Leninist analysis of the state as a weapon of class struggle renders the question still more concrete. Not only are the immediately practical (tactical or ideological) consequences of correct historical knowledge of the bourgeois state made explicit, but the outlines of the proletarian state appear concretely and organically related to the other methods of struggle adopted by the proletariat. The traditional division of labour within the working-class movement (party, trade union, co-operative) is now shown to be inadequate for the present revolutionary struggle of the proletariat. It is necessary to create organs which are able to include the whole proletariat, together with all those exploited under capitalism (peasants and soldiers) in one great mass and lead them into battle. These organs – Soviets – are, within bourgeois society, already essentially weapons of the proletariat organizing itself as a class. Once they exist revolution is on the agenda. For as Marx said: 'The class organization of revolutionary elements presupposes the completion of all the forces of production which can ever develop in the womb of the old society.'

This organization of a whole class has to take up the struggle against the bourgeois state apparatus – whether it wants to or not. There is no choice: either the proletarian Soviets disorganize the bourgeois state apparatus, or the latter succeeds in corrupting the Soviets into a pseudo-existence and in thus destroying them. Either the bourgeoisie undertakes the counter-revolutionary suppression of the revolutionary mass movement and re-establishes 'normal' conditions of 'order', or the proletariat's instrument of rule, its state apparatus – equally one of its struggle – emerges from the Soviets, the instrument of that struggle. Even in 1905, in their earliest and most undeveloped form, the workers' Soviets display this character: *they are an anti-government.* Whereas other organs of the class struggle can make tactical adjustments even during the undisputed rule of the bourgeoisie – in other words, can function in a revolutionary way under such conditions – workers' Soviets are in essential opposition to bourgeois state power as a competing dual government. So when Martov, for example, recognizes the Soviets as organs of struggle but denies their fitness to become a status apparatus, he expunges from his theory precisely the revolution itself – the real proletarian seizure of power. When, on the other hand, individual theoreticians on the extreme left see the workers' Soviets as a permanent class organization and seek to replace party and trade union by them, they in turn reveal their lack of understanding of the difference between revolutionary and non-revolutionary situations, and their confusion as to the actual role of workers' Soviets. For although the mere recognition of the concrete possibility of Soviets points beyond bourgeois society towards the proletarian revolution (the idea of workers' Soviets must therefore be permanently propagated among the proletariat, which must always be prepared to make this revolution), its real existence – if it is not to be a farce – immediately involves a serious struggle for state power, in other words, civil war.

Workers' Soviets as a state apparatus: *that is the state as a weapon in the class struggle of the proletariat.* Because the proletariat fights against bourgeois class rule and strives to create a classless society, the undialectical and therefore unhistorical and unrevolutionary analysis of opportunism concludes that the proletariat must fight against all class rule; in other words, its own form of domination should under no circumstances be an organ of class rule, of class oppression. Taken abstractly this basic viewpoint is utopian, for proletarian rule could never become a reality in this way; taken concretely, however, and applied to the present, it exposes itself as *an ideological capitulation to the bourgeoisie.* From this standpoint the most developed bourgeois form of rule – democracy – appears at a minimum to be an early form of proletarian democracy. At a maximum, however, it appears to be the embodiment of this democracy itself in which it need only be ensured that the majority of the population is won for the 'ideals' of social democracy through peaceful agitation. From this it would follow that the transition from bourgeois to proletarian democracy is not necessarily revolutionary; revolution would be reserved merely for the transition from the backward forms of society to democracy. A revolutionary defence of democracy against social reaction would only be necessary in certain circumstances. (The fact that social democracy has nowhere offered serious resistance to fascist reaction and conducted a revolutionary defence of democracy provides a practical demonstration of the extent to which this mechanistic separation of the proletarian from the bourgeois revolution is wrong and counter-revolutionary.)

Such a standpoint not only eliminates revolution from historical development, represented by all manner of crude or subtle arguments as being an evolution into socialism, *but conceals the bourgeois class character of democracy* from the proletariat. The moment of deception lies in *the undialectical concept of 'the majority'*. Because the representation of the interests of the overwhelming majority of the population is the essence of working-class rule, many workers suffer from the illusion that a purely formal democracy, in which the voice of every citizen is equally valid, is the most suitable instrument for expressing and representing the interests of society as a whole. But this fails to take into account the simple – simple! – detail that men are not just abstract individuals, abstract citizens or isolated atoms within the totality of the state, but are always concrete human beings who occupy specific positions within social production, whose social being (and mediated through it, whose thinking) is determined by this position. The pure democracy of bourgeois society excludes this mediation. It connects the naked and abstract individual directly with the totality of the state, which in this context appears equally abstract. This fundamentally formal character of pure democracy is alone enough to *pulverize bourgeois society politically* – which is not merely an advantage for the bourgeoisie but is precisely the decisive condition of its class rule.

For however much it rests in the last analysis on force, no class rule can, ultimately, maintain itself for long by force alone. 'It is possible,' as Talleyrand once said, 'to do many things with a bayonet, but one cannot sit on one.' *Every minority rule is therefore socially organized both to concentrate the ruling class, equipping it for united and cohesive action, and simultaneously to split and disorganize the oppressed classes*. Where the minority rule of the modern bourgeoisie is concerned, it must always be remembered that the great majority of the population belongs to neither of the two classes which play a decisive part in the class struggle, to neither the proletariat nor the bourgeoisie; and that in addition pure democracy is designed, in social and in class terms, to ensure the bourgeoisie domination over these intermediate strata. (Needless to say, the ideological disorganization of the proletariat is also part of this process. As can be seen most clearly in England and America, the older democracy is in a country and the purer its development, the greater is this ideological disorganization.) Political democracy of this kind is of course by no means enough to achieve this end by itself. It is, however, only the political culmination of a social system whose other elements include the ideological separation of economics and politics, the creation of a bureaucratic state apparatus which gives large sections of the petty bourgeoisie a material and moral interest in the stability of the state, a bourgeois party system, press, schools' system, religion, etc. With a more or less conscious division of labour, all these further the aim of preventing the formation of an independent ideology among the oppressed classes of the population which would correspond to their own class interests; of binding the individual members of these classes as single individuals, as mere 'citizens', to an abstract state reigning over and above all classes; *of disorganizing these classes as classes* and pulverizing them into atoms easily manipulated by the bourgeoisie.

The recognition that Soviets (Soviets of workers, *and* of peasants *and* soldiers) represent proletarian state power, means *the attempt by the proletariat* as the leading revolutionary class *to counteract this process of disorganization*. It must first of all constitute itself as a class. But it must also mobilize those active elements in the intermediate classes which instinctively rebel against the rule of the bourgeoisie, thereby at the same time breaking the material and the ideological influence of the bourgeoisie over them. The more acute opportunists, Otto Bauer for example,[11] have also recognized that the social meaning of the dictatorship of the proletariat, of the dictatorship of Soviets, lies largely *in the radical seizure from the bourgeoisie of the possibility of ideological leadership of these classes – particularly the peasants – and in the conquest of this leadership by the proletariat in the transition period.* The crushing of the bourgeoisie, the smashing of its state apparatus, the destruction of its press, etc., is a vital necessity for the proletarian revolution because the bourgeoisie by no means renounces its efforts to re-establish its economic and political dominance after its initial defeats in the struggle for state power, and for a long time still remains the more powerful class, even under the new conditions of class struggle which result.

With the help of the Soviet system constituting the state, the proletariat therefore conducts the same struggle against capitalist power which it earlier waged for state power. It must destroy the bourgeoisie economically, isolate it politically, and undermine and overthrow it ideologically. But at the same time it must lead to freedom all the other strata of society it has torn from bourgeois leadership. In other words, it is not enough for the proletariat *to fight objectively for the interests* of the other exploited strata. Its state must also serve to overcome by education the inertia and the fragmentation of these strata and *to train them for active and independent participation in the life of the state.* One of the noblest functions of the Soviet system is to bind together those moments of social life which capitalism fragments. Where this fragmentation lies merely in the consciousness of the oppressed classes, they must be made aware of the unity of these moments. The Soviet system, for example, always establishes the indivisible unity of economics and politics by relating the concrete existence of men – their immediate daily interests, etc. – to the essential questions of society as a whole. It also establishes unity in objective reality where bourgeois class interests created the 'division of labour'; above all, the unity of the power 'apparatus' (army, police, government, the law, etc.) and 'the people'. For the armed peasants and workers as embodiments of state power are simultaneously the products of the struggle of the Soviets and the precondition of their existence. Everywhere, the Soviet system does its utmost to relate human activity to general questions concerning the state, the economy, culture, etc., while fighting to ensure that the regulation of all such questions does not become the privilege of an exclusive bureaucratic group remote from social life as a whole. Because the Soviet system, the proletarian state, makes society aware of the real connexions between all moments of social life (and later objectively unites those which are as yet objectively separate – town and country, for example, intellectual and manual labour, etc.), it is a decisive factor in the organization of the proletariat as a class. What existed in the proletariat only as a possibility in capitalist society now becomes a living reality: *the proletariat's real productive energy can only awaken after its seizure of power*. But what is true of the proletariat is also true of the other oppressed strata in bourgeois society. They too can only develop in this context, though they continue to be led even in the new state. But whereas they were led under capitalism because of their inability to become conscious of their own socio-economic destruction, exploitation and oppression, under the leadership of the proletariat they can, on the contrary, not only live according to their own interests, but also develop their hitherto hidden or crippled energies. They are led only in the sense that the limits and direction of their development are determined by the proletariat in its capacity as the leading class of the revolution.

Leadership over the non-proletarian intermediate strata in the proletarian state is therefore, materially, quite different from leadership over them in the bourgeois state. There is also an essential formal difference: *the proletarian state is the first class state in history which acknowledges quite openly and unhypocritically that it is a class state, a repressive apparatus, and an instrument of class struggle*. This relentless honesty and lack of hypocrisy is what makes a real understanding between the proletariat and the other social strata possible in the first place. But above and beyond this, it is an extremely important means of self-education for the proletariat. For however essential it has become to awaken proletarian consciousness to the fact that the era of decisive revolutionary struggles has come – that the struggle for state power, for the leadership of society, has already broken out – it would be dangerous to allow this to become an inflexible and undialectical truth. It would consequently be highly dangerous if the proletariat, having liberated itself from the ideology of pacifist class struggle and having grasped the historical significance and indispensability of force, were now to believe that *all problems* of its rule could in all circumstances be settled *by force*. However, it would be even more dangerous if the proletariat were to imagine that, after it has seized state power, the class struggle ends or at least comes to a standstill. The proletariat must understand that the seizure of state power *is only a phase* of this struggle. After it the struggle only becomes more violent, and it would be quite wrong to maintain that the relationship of forces shifts immediately and decisively in the proletariat's favour. Lenin never ceases to repeat that the bourgeoisie still remains the more powerful class even when the Soviet republic is established, even after the bourgeoisie's own economic expropriation and political suppression. But the relationship of forces does shift in so far as the proletariat takes possession of *a new powerful weapon* of class struggle: *the state*. It is true that the value of this weapon – its ability to undermine, isolate, and destroy the bourgeoisie, to win over and educate the other social strata to cooperation in the workers' and peasants' state, and really to organize the proletariat itself to become the leading class – by no means follows automatically merely from the seizure of state power. Nor does the state inevitably develop as an instrument of struggle merely because power has been seized. The value of the state as a weapon for the proletariat depends on what the proletariat is capable of *making* of it.

The actuality of the revolution expresses itself in the actuality of the problem of the state for the proletariat. With this phase the question of socialism itself at once ceases to be merely an ultimate far-off goal and confronts the proletariat as an immediate task. This tangible proximity of the realization of socialism once again involves, however, a dialectical relationship; it would be fatal for the proletariat if it were to interpret this approach of socialism in a mechanistic and utopian fashion, as its realization merely through the seizure of power (capitalist expropriation, socialization, etc.). Marx made an acute analysis of the transition from capitalism to socialism and pointed out the many bourgeois forms of structure which can only be abolished gradually, in the course of prolonged development. Lenin also draws the dividing-line against utopianism here as firmly as possible. '. . . . Nor I think,' he said, 'has any Communist denied that the term Socialist Soviet Republic implies the determination of Soviet power to achieve the transition to socialism, and not that the new economic system is recognized as a socialist order.' The actuality of the revolution, therefore, undoubtedly means that socialism is now an immediate task of the labour movement; but only in the sense that the establishment of its preconditions must now be fought for day by day and that some of the concrete measures of this daily struggle already constitute concrete advances towards the revolution's fulfilment.

It is precisely at this point – in its criticism of the relationship between Soviets and socialism – that opportunism reveals that it has finally joined the bourgeoisie and become the class enemy of the proletariat. For on the one hand, it regards all the pseudo-concessions which a momentarily alarmed or disorganized bourgeoisie provisionally makes to the proletariat as real steps towards socialism (for instance, the long-defunct 'Socialization Commissions' set up in Germany and Austria in 1918–19).[12] On the other hand, it mocks the Soviet republic for not immediately producing socialism, and for making a bourgeois revolution, proletarian in form and under proletarian leadership (accusations of 'Russia as a peasants' republic', 're-introduction of capitalism', and so on). In both cases, it becomes clear that for opportunists of all shades, *the real enemy* to be fought is *precisely the proletarian revolution itself.* This too is but the consistent extension of the opportunists' attitude to the imperialist war. Similarly, it is only a consistent extension of his criticism of opportunism before and during the war, when Lenin treats its exponents in practice as enemies of the working class in the republic of Soviets.

For *opportunism belongs to the bourgeoisie* – the bourgeoisie whose intellectual and material media must be destroyed and whose whole structure must be disrupted by the dictatorship, so that it should not influence those social strata rendered unstable by their objective class situation. The very actuality of socialism makes this struggle considerably more violent than it was, for instance, at the time of the Bernstein debates. The state as a proletarian weapon in the struggle for socialism and for the suppression of the bourgeoisie is also its weapon for eradicating the opportunist threat to that class struggle of the proletariat which must be pursued with undiminished intensity in the dictatorship.

6. Revolutionary *Realpolitik*

The proletariat seizes state power and establishes its revolutionary dictatorship: the realization of socialism is now a practical task – a problem for which the proletariat is least of all prepared. For the *realpolitik* of the Social Democrats, who consistently treated all questions of the day only as such, unrelated to the whole historical process and without reference to the ultimate problems of the class struggle, thus never pointing realistically and concretely beyond the horizon of bourgeois society, gave socialism once again a utopian character in the eyes of the workers. The separation of the final aim from the movement not only distorts the assessment of everyday questions – those of the movement – but also makes the final aim itself utopian. This reversion to utopianism expresses itself in very different forms. Above all, the utopian conceives socialism not as a process of 'becoming', but as a state of 'being'. In so far as the problems of socialism are raised at all, they are studied only as future economic, cultural and other questions and in terms of the possible technical or other solutions to them when socialism has already entered the phase of its practical realization. How this in the first place becomes socially possible, how it is achieved, or constituted, or what class relations and economic forms the proletariat must confront at the historical moment when it assumes the task of realizing socialism, is not asked. (Similarly Fourier in his time gave a detailed analysis of the organization of the *phalanstères* without being able to show concretely how they were to be established.) Opportunist eclecticism, *the elimination of the dialectic from socialist thought, divorces socialism itself from the historical process of the class struggle.* Those contaminated by it are bound, as a result, to see both the preconditions for the realization of socialism and the problem of this realization from a distorted perspective. This fundamental error goes so deep that it not only affects opportunists, for whom socialism anyway always remains a far-off ultimate goal, but it also leads honest revolutionaries astray. The latter – the majority of the Left in the Second International – saw the revolutionary process, the ongoing struggle for power, clearly enough in the context of practical everyday problems; but they were incapable of seeing the proletariat after the seizure of power – and the resulting concrete problems – from a similar perspective. Here, too, they became utopian.

The admirable realism with which Lenin handled all problems of socialism during the dictatorship of the proletariat, which must win him the respect even of his bourgeois and petty-bourgeois opponents, is therefore only *the consistent application of Marxism*, of historical-dialectical thought, to problems of socialism which have henceforward become topical. In Lenin's writings and speeches – as, incidentally, also in Marx – there is little about *socialism as a completed condition*. There is all the more, however, about the *steps* which can lead to its establishment. For it is impossible for us concretely to imagine the details of socialism as a completed condition. Important as theoretically accurate knowledge of its basic structure is, the significance of this knowledge lies above all in its establishing the criteria by which we can judge the steps we take towards it. Concrete knowledge of socialism is – like socialism itself – a product of the struggle for it; it can only be gained in and through this struggle. All attempts to gain knowledge of socialism which do not follow this path of dialectical interaction with the day-to-day problems of the class struggle make a metaphysic of it, a utopia, something merely contemplative and non-practical.

The aim of Lenin's realism, his *realpolitik*, is therefore *the*

final elimination of all utopianism, the concrete fulfilment of
the content of Marx's programme: a theory become practical, a theory of practice. Lenin handled the problem of
socialism as he had done the problem of the state: he
wrested it from its previous metaphysical isolation and
embourgeoisement *and situated it in the total context of the
problem of the class struggle*. He tested in living history
Marx's genial suggestions, in *The Critique of the Gotha
Programme* and elsewhere, and made them more concrete
and implemented them more fully than Marx had been able
to in his time, despite his genius.

*The problems of socialism are therefore the problems of
economic structure and class relations at the moment when the
proletariat seizes state power*. They arise directly from the
situation in which the working class establishes its dictatorship and can, therefore, only be understood and solved in
relation to its problems. For the same reason they nevertheless contain, in relation to this and all preceding situations, a
fundamentally new quality. Even if all their elements are
rooted in the past, their interconnexion with the maintain-
ance and consolidation of proletarian rule produces new
problems which *could not have existed* either in Marx or in
other earlier theories, and which can only be understood
and solved in the context of this essentially new situation.

Referred back to its context and its foundations, Lenin's
realpolitik thus proves *to be the highest stage yet reached by
the materialist dialectic*. On the one hand, it is a profound
and concrete analysis of the given situation, its economic
structure and class relations, strictly Marxist in its simplicity
and sobriety; on the other hand, it is a lucid awareness of all
new tendencies arising from this situation, unclouded by
any theoretical prejudice or utopian fancies. These apparently simple qualities, rooted as they are in the nature of the
materialist dialectic – in itself a theory of history – are by no
means easy to attain. The customary ways of thinking under
capitalism have given everyone – particularly those inclined
to systematic study – the tendency always to want to explain

the new completely in terms of the old, today entirely in terms of yesterday. (Revolutionary utopianism is an attempt to pull oneself up by one's own bootstraps, to land with one jump in a completely new world, instead of understanding, with the help of the dialectic, the dialectical evolution of the new from the old.) 'That is why,' said Lenin, 'very many people are misled by the term state capitalism. To avoid this we must remember the fundamental thing that state capitalism in the form we have here is not dealt with in any theory, or in any books, for the simple reason that all the usual concepts connected with this term are associated with bourgeois rule in capitalist society. Our society is one which has left the rails of capitalism, but has not yet got on to new rails.'[13]

But what real concrete environment for the achievement of socialism did the Russian proletariat find once it attained power? First, a relatively developed monopoly capitalism in a state of collapse as a result of the world war, in a backward peasant country where the peasantry could only liberate itself from the shackles of feudal survivals in alliance with the proletarian revolution. Second, a hostile capitalist environment outside Russia, ready to throw itself upon the new workers' and peasants' state with all the resources at its disposal, strong enough to crush it militarily or economically were it not itself divided by the ever-increasing contradictions of imperialist capitalism, which offer the proletariat the constant opportunity to exploit imperialism's internal and other rivalries for its own ends. (This is naturally to indicate only the two chief problem areas; not even these can be discussed exhaustively in these few pages.)

The material basis of socialism as a higher economic form replacing capitalism can only be provided by the reorganization and higher development of industry, its adjustment to the needs of the working class, its transformation in the direction of an ever more meaningful existence (abolition of the opposition between town and country, intellectual and manual labour, etc.). The condition of this material basis therefore determines the possibilities and path of its concrete realization. In this respect – already in 1917, before the seizure of power – Lenin gave a clear exposition of the economic situation and the proletarian tasks which resulted from it: 'The dialectic of history is such that war, by extraordinarily expediting the transformation of monopoly capitalism, has *thereby* extraordinarily advanced mankind towards socialism. Imperialist war is the eve of socialist revolution. And this not only because the horrors of war give rise to proletarian revolt – no revolt can bring about socialism unless the economic conditions for socialism are ripe – but because state-monopoly capitalism is a complete *material* preparation for socialism, the threshold of socialism, a rung on the ladder of history between which and the rung called socialism *there are no intermediate rungs*.' As a result, 'socialism is merely state-monopoly capitalism *which is made to serve the interests of the whole people* and has to that extent *ceased* to be capitalist monopoly'. Further, he writes, at the beginning of 1918: ' ... In the present circumstances, state capitalism would mean a step forward in our Soviet republic. If, for example, state capitalism firmly established itself here after six months, that would be a mighty achievement and the surest guarantee that, after a year, socialism would be finally and irrevocably established here.'

These passages have been quoted in particular detail to refute widespread bourgeois and social democratic myths according to which, after the failure of 'doctrinaire Marxist' attempts to introduce communism 'at one sweep', Lenin compromised and, 'clever realist that he was', deviated from his original political line. The historical truth is the opposite. So-called 'War Communism' – about which Lenin said: 'It was a makeshift' and: 'It was the war and the ruin that forced us into War Communism. It was not, and could not be, a policy that corresponded to the economic tasks of the proletariat' – was itself a deviation from the path along which the development of socialism was to have run, according to his theoretical predictions. Of course, it was determined by the internal and external civil war and was therefore unavoidable, but it was still only a makeshift. And, according to Lenin, it would have been fatal for the proletariat to have been ignorant of this character of War Communism, let alone to have thought of it as a real step towards socialism, as did many sincere revolutionaries who were not on his theoretical level.

The crux of the matter is, therefore, not to what extent the outward forms of the economy are in themselves socialist in character, but exclusively to what extent the proletariat succeeds in *actually* controlling heavy industry – the economic apparatus of which it took possession when it seized power and which is at the same time the basis of its own social existence – and to what extent it succeeds in *really* using this control to further its own class aims. No matter how much the context of these aims and the corresponding means for their realization changes, their general basis still remains the same: to pursue the class struggle by leading the vacillating intermediate strata (particularly the peasants) on the decisive front – the front against the bourgeoisie. And here it should never be forgotten that, despite its first victory, the proletariat still remains the weaker class and will remain so for a long time – until revolution is victorious on a world scale. Economically its struggle must therefore be based on two principles: firstly to stop as quickly and completely as possible the destruction of heavy industry by war and civil war, for without this material basis the proletariat is bound to be destroyed; secondly to regulate all problems of production and distribution to the maximum satisfaction of the material needs of the peasantry so that the alliance established with the proletariat by the revolutionary solution of the agrarian question can be maintained. The means for the realization of these aims change according to the circumstances. Their gradual implementation is, however, the only way to maintain the rule of the proletariat – the first precondition of socialism.

The class struggle between bourgeoisie and proletariat is therefore also waged with undiminished intensity on the internal economic front. Small-scale industry, the abolition and 'socialization' of which is pure utopianism at this stage, 'is continuously, day by day, hour by hour, in an elemental sense and on a mass scale, creating capitalism and a bourgeoisie'. The question is which of the two is going to gain the upper hand: this re-emerging and re-accumulating bourgeoisie or heavy state industry controlled by the proletariat? The proletariat must risk this competition if it does not in the long run want to risk the loosening of its alliance with the peasants by strangling small-scale industry, trade, etc. (which is in practice an illusion anyway). In addition, the bourgeoisie offers yet more competition in the form of foreign capital or concessions. Paradoxically, this development (whatever bourgeois intentions) can, by strengthening the economic power of heavy industry, become an objective economic aid of the proletariat. Thus 'an alliance is born against small-scale industry'. At the same time, of course, concessionary capital's normal tendency gradually to transform the proletarian state into a capitalist economy must be vigorously opposed (by restrictions on concessions, monopoly of exports, etc.).

It is impossible in these few remarks to attempt even the merest outline of Lenin's economic policy. They are intended only as examples to allow *the theoretical basis* of his political *principle* to emerge with some degree of clarity. This principle is: in a universe of open and secret enemies and hesitant allies, to maintain the rule of the proletariat at all costs. In the same way, his basic political principle before the seizure of power was to discover those factors in the tangle of interwoven social tendencies of declining capitalism whose exploitation by the proletariat was capable of transforming it into the leading – the ruling – class in society. Lenin held to this principle unshakeably and uncompromisingly throughout his whole life. In the same implacable way, he held to it *as a dialectical principle*, in the sense that 'the basis of the Marxist dialectic is that all limits in nature and in history are simultaneously determinate and mutable, and that there is *not a single* phenomenon which, under certain conditions, cannot be transformed into its opposite'. The dialectic therefore demands 'a comprehensive examination of the relevant social phenomena in the course of their development, and the reduction of all exterior and visible manifestations to their basic, motivating forces – to the development of the forces of production and of the class struggle'. Lenin's greatness as a dialectician consisted in his ability clearly to see the basic principles of the dialectic, the development of the productive forces and the class struggle always in their innermost essence, concretely, without abstract prejudices, but also without being fetishistically confused by superficialities. He always related all phenomena to their ultimate basis – *to the concrete actions of concrete (in other words class-conditioned) men in accordance with their real class interests*. Only in the light of this principle do the legends of Lenin 'the clever power politician' and the 'master of compromise' collapse to reveal the true Lenin, the theorist who consistently developed the Marxist dialectic.

Above all, when defining the concept of compromise, any suggestion that it is a question of knack, of cleverness, of an astute fraud, must be rejected. 'We must,' said Lenin, 'decisively reject those who think that politics consists of little tricks, sometimes bordering on deceit. *Classes cannot be deceived.*' For Lenin, therefore, compromise means *that the true developmental tendencies of classes* (and possibly of nations – for instance, where an oppressed people is concerned), which under specific circumstances and for a certain period run parallel in determinate areas with the interests of the proletariat, are exploited to the advantage of *both*.

Naturally, compromises can also be a form of class struggle against the decisive enemy of the working class – the bourgeoisie (one only need consider Soviet Russia's relations with imperialist countries). Opportunist theoreticians also fasten on to this special form of compromise, partly to build Lenin up, or to run him down, as an 'undogmatic power politician', and partly to find by doing so a camouflage for their own compromises. We have already pointed out the weaknesses of the first argument. To judge the second – as with every dialectical question – the total concrete environment of the compromise must be taken into account. It now becomes immediately clear that Lenin's type of compromise and opportunist compromise *are based on diametrically opposed assumptions*. Whether consciously or unconsciously, social democratic tactics are based on the belief that the real revolution is still a long way off, that the objective preconditions of social revolution do not yet exist, that the proletariat is not yet ideologically mature enough for revolution, the party and trade unions are still too weak, and that *for these reasons* the proletariat must make compromises with the bourgeoisie. In other words, the more the subjective and objective preconditions of social revolution are present, the more 'purely' will the proletariat be able to fulfil its class aims. So the reverse of practical compromise is often great radicalism – absolute 'purity' of principle in relation to the 'ultimate goal'. (It goes without saying that we can in this context only consider the theories of those Social Democrats who still to some extent believe in the concept of class struggle. For those who do not, compromises are obviously no longer compromises but the natural collaboration of various professional strata for the good of the whole community.)

For Lenin, on the other hand, *compromise is a direct and logical consequence of the actuality of the revolution*. If this actuality defines the basic character of the whole era, if the revolution can break out at any moment – either in a single country or on a world scale – without this moment ever being exactly determinable; if the revolutionary character of the whole epoch is revealed in the ever-increasing decay of bourgeois society, which results in the most varied tendencies continuously interchanging and criss-crossing, then the proletariat cannot begin and complete its revolution under 'favourable' conditions of its own choosing, and must always exploit all those tendencies which – however temporarily – further the revolution or which can at least weaken its enemies. Earlier we quoted some passages from Lenin which showed how few illusions he had – even before the seizure of power – about the speed with which socialism could be realized. The following passage from one of his last essays, written after the period of 'compromises', still shows just as clearly that, for Lenin, this prediction never meant the postponement of revolutionary action: 'Napoleon wrote: "*On s'engage et puis . . . on voit.*" Rendered freely this means: "First engage in a serious battle and then see what happens." Well, we did first engage in a serious battle in October 1917, and then saw such details of development (from the standpoint of world history they were certainly details) as the Brest Peace, the New Economic Policy, and so forth.'

The Leninist theory and tactic of compromise is, therefore, only the objective, logical corollary of the Marxist – dialectical – historical recognition that, although men make their own history, they cannot do so in circumstances chosen by themselves. This follows from the knowledge that history always creates new conditions; that therefore moments in history when different tendencies intersect never recur in the same form; that tendencies can be judged favourable to the revolution today which are a mortal danger to it tomorrow, and vice versa. Thus, on 1 September 1917, Lenin wanted to offer the Mensheviks and Social Revolutionaries a compromise, a common action, based on the old Bolshevik slogan, 'All Power to the Soviets'. But already on 17 September he writes: '. . . Perhaps it is already too late to offer a compromise. Perhaps the few days in which a peaceful development was *still* possible have passed *too*. Yes, to all appearances, they have already passed.' The application of this theory to Brest-Litovsk, to the economic concessions, is self-evident.

The extent to which the whole Leninist theory of compromise has its base in his fundamental concept of the actuality of the revolution is possibly made even clearer by the thoretical battles he fought against the left wing of his own party (on a Russian scale after the First Revolution, in 1905, and at the time of the peace of Brest-Litovsk, and on a European scale in 1920 and 1921). In all these debates, *the slogan of left-wing radicalism was the rejection in principle of any compromise*. Lenin's polemic shows very substantially that this rejection contains *an evasion of decisive struggles*, behind which lies *a defeatist attitude towards the revolution*. For the genuine revolutionary situation – and, according to Lenin, this is the principal feature of our age – expresses itself in the fact that there are no areas of the class struggle in which revolutionary (or counter-revolutionary) possibilities are not present. The genuine revolutionary, the revolutionary who knows that we live in a revolutionary period and who draws the practical conclusions from the knowledge, must therefore always see the totality of socio-historic reality from this standpoint and, in the interests of the revolution, must rigorously consider all events – big or small, normal or untoward – according and *only* according to their importance for it. In sometimes referring to 'left-wing Radicalism' as 'left-wing Opportunism', Lenin very rightly and profoundly indicated *the common historical perspective* of these two otherwise mutually antagonistic tendencies, for one of which any compromise is taboo, while for the other it represents the principle of *realpolitik* in opposition to 'strict adherence to dogmatic principles'. He pointed out, in other words, that both were pessimistic regarding the proximity and actuality of the proletarian revolution. By thus rejecting both tendencies from the same principle, Lenin makes it clear that compromise for him and compromise for opportunists are *only verbally the same*: the word as used by each refers to fundamentally different premisses and therefore covers *two fundamentally different concepts*.

A proper understanding of what Lenin meant by compromise, on what he theoretically founded its tactics, is not only fundamental to a correct understanding of his method, but is also of far-reaching practical importance. For Lenin compromise *is only possible in dialectical interaction with strict adherence to the principles and method of Marxism*; it always indicates the next realistic step towards the realization of Marxist theory. Therefore, however sharply this theory and tactic are to be distinguished from rigid adherence to 'pure' principles, they must also be totally separated from all unprincipled, schematic *realpolitik*. In other words, for Lenin, it is not enough for a concrete situation – the specific balance of forces determining a compromise, and the tendency of the necessary development of the proletarian movement guiding its orientation – to be properly recognized and evaluated *in its reality*. He regards it as *an enormous practical danger* for the labour movement if such a correct appreciation of the actual facts is not related to a generally correct appreciation *of the whole historical process*. Thus, while acknowledging the practical attitude of the German Communists to the projected 'Workers' Government' after the crushing of the Kapp Putsch – so-called 'loyal opposition' – to be correct, he simultaneously censured this tactic most severely on the grounds that it was based on a theoretically false historical perspective, full of democratic illusions.[14]

The dialectically correct fusion of the general and the specific, the recognition of the general (in the sense of general historical tendencies) *in* the specific (in the concrete situation), and the resulting concretization of theory, is therefore the basis of this theory of compromise. Those who see Lenin merely as a clever or perhaps even brilliant exponent of *realpolitik* thoroughly misunderstand the essence of his method. But those who think that they can find in his decisions 'formulas' and 'precepts' for correct and practical action applicable everywhere misunderstand him even more deeply. Lenin never laid down 'general rules' which could be 'applied' in a number of different cases. His 'truths' grow from a concrete analysis of the concrete situation based on a dialectical approach to history. Only a caricature, vulgar Leninism can result from a mechanical 'generalization' of his insights and decisions – as shown, for instance, by those Hungarian Communists who tried schematically to imitate the Brest-Litovsk Peace in a totally different context, when replying to the Clemenceau Note in Summer 1919.[15] For, as Marx sharply censured Lassalle: '. ... The dialectical method is wrongly applied. Hegel never called the subsumption of a mass of different "cases" under a general principle dialectical.'

But the need to take into account all existing tendencies in every concrete situation by no means implies that all are of equal weight when decisions are taken. On the contrary, *every situation contains a central problem* the solution of which determines both the answer to the other questions raised simultaneously by it and the key to the further development of all social tendencies in the future. 'You must,' said Lenin, 'be able at each particular moment to find the particular link in the chain which you must grasp with all your might in order to hold the whole chain and to prepare firmly for the transition to the next link; the order of the links, their form, the manner in which they are linked together, the way they differ from each other in the historical chain of events, are not as simple and not as meaningless as those in an ordinary chain made by a smith.' Only the Marxist dialectic, by the concrete analysis of the concrete situation, can establish what fact at a given moment of social life acquires this significance. Its leitmotive is the revolutionary concept of society *as a continuously developing totality*. For only this relation to the totality gives the relevant decisive link this significance: it must be grasped because it is only by doing so that the totality itself can be grasped. Lenin gives the problem particularly sharp and concrete emphasis again in one of his last essays, when he speaks of co-operatives and points out that 'much that was fantastic, even romantic, even banal in the dreams of the old co-operators is now becoming unvarnished reality'. 'Strictly speaking,' he says, 'there is *"only"* one thing we have left to do and that is to make our people so "enlightened" that they understand all the advantages of everybody participating in the work of the co-operatives, and organize this participation. *"Only"* that. There are now no other devices needed to advance socialism. But to achieve this "only", there must be a veritable revolution – the entire people must go through a period of cultural development.'

It is unfortunately impossible to analyse the whole essay in detail here. Such an analysis – and, for that matter, an analysis of any one of Lenin's theoretical insights – would show how the whole is always contained in each link of the chain; that the criterion of true Marxist politics always consists in extracting and concentrating the greatest energy upon those moments in the historical process which – at any given instance or phase – contain within them this relationship to the present whole and to the question of development central for the future – to the future in its practical and tangible totality. Therefore, this energetic seizure of the next decisive link of the chain by no means entails the extraction of its moment from the totality at the expense of the other moments in it. On the contrary, it means that, *once related to this central problem*, all other moments of the historical process can thereby be correctly understood and solved. The connexion of all problems with one another is not loosened by this approach; it is strengthened and made more concrete.

Those moments are brought into the open by history, by the objective development of productive forces. But it depends on the proletariat whether and how far it is able to recognize, grasp and thereby *influence their further development*. The fundamental and already oft-quoted Marxist axiom that men make their own history acquires an ever-increasing importance in the revolutionary period after the seizure of state power, even if its dialectical counterpart, which stresses that the circumstances are not freely chosen, is an essential part of its truth. This means in practice that *the party's role in a revolution* – the masterly idea of the early Lenin – *is even more important and more decisive* in the period of transition to socialism than in the preparatory period. For the greater the proletariat's active influence in determining the course of history, the more fateful – both in the good and the bad sense – its decisions become both for itself and for the whole of mankind, the more important it is to preserve the only compass for these wild and stormy seas – *proletarian class consciousness* – in its purest form and to help this unique guide in the struggle to achieve even greater clarity. This concept of the proletarian party's active historical role is a fundamental tenet of Lenin's theory and therefore of his politics which he tired neither of emphasizing again and again, nor of stressing its importance for practical decisions. Thus at the Eleventh Congress of the Russian Communist Party, when attacking the opponents of state capitalism, he said: 'State capitalism is capitalism which we shall be able to restrain, and the limits of which we shall be able to fix. This state capitalism is connected with the state, and the state is the workers, the advanced section of the workers, the vanguard. We are the state. . . . And it rests with us to determine what this state capitalism is to be.'

That is why every turning-point in the development of socialism is always simultaneously *a critical internal party matter*. It is a regrouping of forces, the adjustment of the party organization to new tasks: the *influencing* of society in the direction dictated by a careful and accurate analysis of the whole historical process from the class standpoint of the proletariat. That is why the party occupies the summit of the hierarchy of the decisive forces in the state *which we constitute*. Because the revolution can only be victorious on a world scale, because it is only as a world proletariat that the working class can truly become a class, the party itself is incorporated and subordinated as a section within the highest organ of proletarian revolution, the Communist International. The mechanistic rigidity characterizing all opportunist and bourgeois thought will always see insoluble contradictions in such a relationship. It cannot understand how, even after they have 'returned to capitalism', the Bolsheviks still uphold the old party structure and the 'undemocratic' dictatorship of the party. Nor how the Communist International does not for a moment abandon the world revolution, striving to use every means at its disposal to prepare and organize it, while the Russian workers' state simultaneously tries to promote peace with the imperialist powers and the maximum participation of imperialist capitalism in Russia's economic construction. It cannot understand why the party stubbornly preserves its internal cohesion and most energetically pursues its ideological and organizational consolidation, while the economic policy of the Soviet Republic anxiously safeguards from any erosion that alliance with the peasants to which it owes its existence – thus seeming to opportunists increasingly to be a peasant state, sacrificing its proletarian character, etc., etc. The mechanistic rigidity of undialectical thought is incapable of understanding *that these contradictions are the objective, essential contradictions of the present period*; that the Russian Communist Party's policy, Lenin's policy, is only contradictory in so far as *it seeks and finds the dialectically correct solutions to the objective contradictions of its own social existence.*

Thus the analysis of Lenin's policy always leads us back to the basic question of dialectical method. His whole life-work is the consistent application of the Marxist dialectic to the ever-changing, perpetually new phenomena of an immense period of transition. But because the dialectic is not a finished theory to be applied mechanically to all the phenomena of life *but only exists as theory in and through this application*, Lenin's practice gives it a broader, more complete and *theoretically more developed* form than it had when he inherited it from Marx and Engels.

It is therefore completely justifiable to speak of *Leninism as a new phase* in the development of the materialist dialectic. Lenin not only re-established the purity of Marxist doctrine after decades of decline and distortion by vulgar Marxism, but he developed, concretized, and matured the method itself. If it is now the task of Communists to continue in Lenin's footsteps, this can only be fruitful if they attempt to establish the same active relation to him as he had to Marx. The nature and content of this activity are determined by the problems and tasks with which history confronts Marxism. Its success is determined by the degree of proletarian class-consciousness in the party which leads the working class. Leninism means that the theory of historical materialism has moved still nearer the daily battles of the proletariat, that it has become more practical than it could be at the time of Marx. The Leninist tradition can therefore only mean the undistorted and flexible preservation of this living and enlivening, growing and creative function of historical materialism. That is why – we repeat – Lenin must be studied by Communists in the same spirit as he studied Marx. He must be studied in order to learn how to apply the dialectic; to learn how to discover, by concrete analysis of concrete situations, the specific in the general and the general in the specific; to see in the novelty of a situation what connects it with former developments; to observe the perpetually new phenomena constantly produced under the laws of historical development; to detect the part in the whole and the whole in the part; to find in historical necessity the moment of activity and in activity the connexion with historical necessity.

Leninism represents a hitherto unprecedented degree of concrete, unschematic, unmechanistic, purely praxis-oriented thought. To preserve *this* is the task of the Leninist. But, in the historical process, only what develops in living fashion can be preserved. *Such a preservation* of the Leninist tradition is today the noblest duty of all serious believers in the dialectic as a weapon in the class struggle of the proletariat.

Postscript 1967

This small book was set down immediately after Lenin's death, without any special preparation, to satisfy the spontaneous need to establish theoretically what then seemed to me essential – the spiritual centre of Lenin's personality. Hence the subtitle 'A Study on the Unity of his Thought'. It indicates that my concern was not to reproduce his objective theoretical system, but rather to give an account of the objective and subjective forces that made this systematization and its embodiment in Lenin's person and actions possible. There was no question of even attempting to analyse the full breadth of this dynamic unity in his life and work.

The relatively great contemporary interest in such writings is above all a sign of the times. Since the emergence of a Marxist critique of the Stalin era there has also been renewed interest in the oppositional tendencies of the twenties. This is understandable, if from a theoretical and objective standpoint very much exaggerated. For, however false the solutions offered by Stalin and his followers to the developing crisis of the Revolution, there is no question that anyone else at that time could have provided an analysis or perspective which could have given a theoretical guide-line to the problems of the later phases as well. A fruitful contribution to the renaissance of Marxism requires a purely historical treatment of the twenties as a past period of the revolutionary working-class movement which is now entirely closed. This is the only way to make its experiences and lessons properly relevant to the essentially new phase of the present. But Lenin, as is the rule with great men, so embodied his age that the results, but especially the method, of what he said and did can still retain a definite contemporaneity even under very changed circumstances.

This work is a pure product of the mid twenties. As a document of how a not inconsiderable group of Marxists saw Lenin's personality and mission, his place in the course of world events, it is therefore certainly not without interest. But it must always be remembered that its ideas were determined more by the conceptions of the period – including their illusions and extravagances – than was Lenin's own theoretical life work. The first sentence itself demonstrates the prejudices of the time: 'Historical materialism is the theory of the proletarian revolution.' No doubt this is the expression of an important determinant of historical materialism. But equally certainly it is not the only, not *the* determination of its essence. And Lenin, for whom the actuality of the proletarian revolution formed the thread of thought and practice, would have raised the most passionate protest against any attempt to reduce to a single dimension and to cramp the real and methodological wealth – the social universality – of historical materialism, by such a 'definition'.

Criticism in the spirit of Lenin could be applied to a great many passages in this little book. I shall limit myself simply to indicating the legitimacy and direction of such criticism, for I hope that sober, thoughtful readers will themselves establish a critical distance. I think it important to emphasize where the outlook I drew from Lenin led to conclusions which still retain a certain methodological validity as moments in the elimination of Stalinism; where, in other words, the author's devotion to Lenin's person and work did not, after all, go astray. For certain of my comments on Lenin's behaviour contain, implicitly, some accurate criticism of Stalin's later development, which was then still hidden except for fleeting glimpses in Zinoviev's leadership of the Comintern. For example, the increasing sclerosis under Stalin of all organizational problems: whatever the situation at the time, whatever the demands of politics, the party organization was made into an immutable fetish – even using an appeal to Lenin's authority. I cite here Lenin's warning: 'Political questions cannot be mechanically separated from organization questions', and the following comment made in the spirit of just such a Leninist political dynamic: 'Therefore, all dogmatism in theory and all sclerosis in organization are disastrous for the party. For as Lenin said: "Every new form of struggle which brings new perils and sacrifices inevitably 'disorganizes' an organization ill-prepared for the new form of struggle." It is the party's task to pursue its necessary path openly and consciously – above all in relation to itself – so that it may transform itself before the danger of disorganization becomes acute, and by this transformation promote the transformation and advance of the masses.' At the time, of course, this was objectively only a rearguard action of the concrete revolutionary ferment of the great years against the encroachment of bureaucratic and mechanical uniformity.

But if dogmatic conformity in all areas is to be successfully resisted today, the conclusions of the twenties will only yield fruitful impulses by a detour, if they are recognized to be part of the past. For this it is indispensable that the differences between the twenties and the period we are now living in should be clearly and critically realized. It goes without saying that we must also approach Lenin's work with a similar critical clarity. For those who have no wish to build out of this work some 'infallible' collection of dogmas, this does not in the least reduce his secular greatness. For example, we know today that the Leninist thesis that imperialist development necessarily leads to world war has lost its general validity in the present. Of course, only the inevitability of this development has been invalidated; but its reduction to a possibility changes its theoretical meaning as well as – especially – its practical consequences. Similarly, Lenin generalized the experiences of the First World War – 'What a mystery is the birth of war' – to future imperialist wars, where the future produced a quite different picture.

I have given such examples precisely to reveal Lenin's true singularity, which has nothing, absolutely nothing to do with the bureaucratic ideal of a Stalinist monument of infallibility. Naturally, an account of Lenin's true greatness is far beyond the scope of this book, which is much more time-bound than its subject. In the last years of his life Lenin foresaw the approaching end of the period ushered in by 1917 with incomparably greater clarity than did this study of him.

Nevertheless, the book now and then gives a hint of Lenin's true spiritual stature, and I should like to start my exposition from these glimmers of the truth which I perceived then. It establishes that Lenin was no specialist in economics compared with his contemporaries, Hilferding and, above all, Rosa Luxemburg. But in judging the period as a whole he was far superior to them. This 'superiority – and this is an unparalleled achievement – consists in his concrete articulation of the economic theory of imperialism with every political problem of the present epoch, thereby making the economics of the new phase a guideline for all concrete action in the resultant decisive conjuncture.' Many of his contemporaries noted this as well; friend or foe, they often spoke of his tactical skill and grasp of *realpolitik*.

But such judgements miss the kernel of the matter. It was much more a purely theoretical superiority in the assessment of the process as a whole. Lenin gave this superiority a theoretically deep and rich basis. His so-called *realpolitik* was never that of an empirical pragmatist, but the practical culmination of an essentially theoretical attitude. With him its terminus was always an understanding of the socio-historical particularity of the given situation in which action had to be taken. For Lenin as a Marxist 'the concrete analysis of the concrete situation is not an opposite of "pure" theory, but – on the contrary – it is the culmination of genuine theory, its consummation – the point where it breaks into practice'. Without any exaggeration it may be said that Marx's final, definitive thesis on Feuerbach – 'The philosophers have only *interpreted* the world in different ways; the point, however, is to change it' – found its most perfect embodiment in Lenin and his work. Marx himself threw down the challenge and answered it in the realm of theory. He gave an interpretation of social reality which provided the appropriate theoretical basis for changing it. But it was only with Lenin that this theoretico-practical essence of the new *Weltanschauung* became – without abandoning or suppressing theory – actively embodied in historical reality.

Of course, this book makes only a modest contribution to an understanding of Lenin's true character. It lacks a theoretically deep broad foundation. It also fails to give an idea of Lenin as a human type. I can only indicate this here. In the chain of democratic revolutions in the modern age the types of the revolutionary leader have always been polarized; figures such as Danton and Robespierre embodied these polar images both in reality and in great literature (one thinks of Georg Büchner). Even the great orators of the workers' revolution, such as Lassalle and Trotsky, have certain Dantonesque features.

With Lenin, for the first time something completely new appears, a *tertium datur* to both extremes. Down to his spontaneous instincts, Lenin has the fidelity to principle of the previous great ascetics of revolution – but without a shadow of asceticism in his character. He is lively and humorous; he enjoys everything life offers, from hunting, fishing and playing chess to reading Pushkin and Tolstoy; and he is devoted to real men. This loyalty to principle can become rock-hard implacability in the Civil War; but it never implies any hatred. Lenin fights institutions – and, naturally, the men who represent them – if necessary to their complete destruction. But he treats this as an inevitable, objective necessity which is humanly deplorable, but from which he cannot withdraw in the actually given concrete struggle. Gorky records Lenin's characteristic comments on listening to Beethoven's *Appassionata*: ' "The *Appassionata* is the most beautiful thing I know; I could listen to it every day. What wonderful, almost super-human music! I always think with pride – perhaps it is naïve of me – what marvellous things human beings can do." Then he screwed up his eyes, smiled, and added regretfully, "But I can't listen to music too often. It works on my nerves so that I would rather talk foolishness and stroke the heads of people who live in this filthy hell and can still create such beauty. But now is not the time to stroke heads – you might get your hand bitten off. We must hit people mercilessly on the head, even when we are ideally against any violence between men. Oh! our work is hellishly difficult." '

Even with such a spontaneous emotional utterance of Lenin's, it should be clear that this is no outbreak of his instincts against his 'way of life', but that here too he is strictly consistent with the imperatives of his world view. Decades before this eposide the young Lenin was writing polemics against the Narodniks and their Legal Marxist critics. Analysing the latter, he pointed out the objectivism of their proof 'of the necessity of a given series of facts', and how easy it was as a result to risk finding themselves 'in the position of apologists for these facts'. For him, the only solution was the greater consistency of Marxism in its grasp of objective reality, the uncovering of the real social roots of the facts themselves. The Marxist's superiority over the mere objectivist lies in this consistency; he 'applies his objectivism both more profoundly and more rigorously'. Only this superior objectivity can be the source of what Lenin calls commitment – 'to commit yourself, when evaluating any event, directly and openly to the standpoint of a specific social group'. The subjective attitude thus always arises from objective reality and returns to it.

This can produce conflicts if the contradictions of reality reach a point of mutually exclusive opposition, and every committed man has to settle such conflicts for himself. But there is a fundamental difference between the conflict of convictions and feelings rooted in reality – in an individual's relations – and the man in conflict who feels his own inner existence as a human being in danger. The latter is never true of Lenin. Hamlet says in highest praise of Horatio:

> . . . And blest are those,
> Whose blood and judgement are so well commingled,
> That they are not a pipe of Fortune's finger
> To sound what stops she please.

Blood and judgement: both their opposition and their unity only derive from the biological sphere as the immediate and general basis of human existence. Concretely, both express a man's social being in his harmony or dissonance with the historical moment, in practice and in theory. Blood and judgement were well mixed in Lenin because he oriented his knowledge of society at any moment to the action that was socially necessary at the time, and because his practice always followed necessarily from the sum and system of the true insights accumulated hitherto.

Thus there was in Lenin no trace of what might remotely have appeared as self-satisfaction. Success never made him vain, failure never made him down-hearted. He insisted that there was no situation to which man could not have a practical reaction. He was one of those great men who – precisely in their life's practice – achieved much, including the most essential. Nevertheless – or perhaps therefore – almost no one else wrote of possible or actual failures so soberly, with so little pathos: 'The intelligent man is not one who makes no mistakes. There are no such men and cannot be. The intelligent man is one who makes no fundamental mistakes and who knows how to correct his errors swiftly and painlessly.' This highly prosaic comment on the art of action is a more adequate expression of his essential attitude than any high-flown confession of faith. His life was one of permanent action, of continuous struggle in a world in which he was profoundly convinced that there was no situation without a solution, for himself or his opponents. The leitmotive of his life was, accordingly: always be armed ready for action – for correct action.

Lenin's sober simplicity had therefore an overpowering effect on the masses. Again in contrast to the earlier type of great revolutionary, he was an unequalled tribune of the people, without a trace of rhetoric (compare Lassalle or Trotsky). In private as much as in public life he had a deep aversion to all phrase-mongering, bombast, or exaggeration. It is again significant that he gave this human, political distaste for anything 'exorbitant' an objective, philosophical basis: '... Any truth ... if exaggerated, or if extended beyond the limits of its actual applicability can be reduced to an absurdity, and is even bound to become an absurdity under these conditions.'

This means that, for Lenin, even the most general philosophical categories were never of abstract contemplative generality; they were constantly geared to practice, as vehicles of theoretical preparation for it. In the debate on trade unions he opposed Bukharin's double-edged, mediating eclecticism by relying on the category of the totality. It is particularly characteristic of Lenin that he should apply a philosophical category in this way: 'If we are to have a true knowledge of an object we must look at and experience all its facets, its connexions and "mediacies". That is something we cannot ever hope to achieve completely, but the rule of comprehensiveness is a safeguard against mistakes and rigidity.' It is instructive to see here how an abstract philosophical category, deepened by epistemological provisos governing its application, serves directly as an imperative to correct practice.

This attitude of Lenin's is if possible even more clearly expressed in the debate over the peace of Brest-Litovsk. It is now an historical commonplace that he was correct in his *realpolitik* as against the Left Communists who, on internationalist grounds, argued for the support of the coming

German Revolution with a revolutionary war, thus gambling with the very existence of the Russian Soviet Republic. But Lenin's correct practice here rested on a deep theoretical analysis of the particularity of the development of the revolution as a whole. The priority of the world revolution over any single event, he said, was a genuine (and therefore practical) truth, 'if we are not to ignore the long and difficult road to the total victory of socialism'. But, with respect to the theoretical particularity of that concrete situation, he added that 'any abstract truth becomes a catch-word if it is applied to *each and every concrete situation*'. The difference between truth and revolutionary phraseology as the basis of practice is, therefore, that whereas the former derives from the exact state of the revolutionary struggle necessary and possible at the time, the latter does not. The noblest feelings, the most selfless devotion, become mere phrases if the theoretical essence of the situation (its particularity) allows no genuine revolutionary practice. Such a practice does not necessarily have to be successful. In the 1905 Revolution, Lenin passionately opposed Plechanov's verdict on the defeat of the armed uprising in Moscow, that 'we should not have taken up arms', on the grounds that this defeat itself furthered the revolutionary process as a whole. Any analogy, any confusion of the abstract with the concrete, of the universal with the actual, leads immediately to empty phrases; for example, the comparison of France in 1792–3 and Russia in 1918 which was frequently employed during the Brest-Litovsk debate. Similarly, when the German Communists drafted some highly intelligent, self-critical theses after the Kapp Putsch in 1920, as guide-lines for the eventuality of the recurrence of such a putsch, Lenin is reported to have asked them: How do you know that German Reaction will repeat such a coup at all?

Such responses have behind them Lenin's life of continuous self-education. At the outbreak of war in 1914, after a series of adventures with the police, he landed up in Switzerland. Once arrived, he decided that his first task was to make the best use of this 'holiday' and to study Hegel's *Logic*. Similarly, when he was living illegally in a worker's house after the events of July 1917, he remarked how the latter praised the bread before the mid-day meal: 'So "they" don't even dare give us bad bread now.' Lenin was astonished and delighted by this 'class appraisal of the July days'. He thought of his own complex analyses of this event and the tasks they posed. 'As for bread, I, who had not known want, did not give it a thought. ... The mind approaches the foundation of every-thing, the class struggle for bread, through political analysis by an extremely complex and devious path.' Through his life, Lenin was always learning; whether it was from Hegel's *Logic* or from the opinion of a worker on bread.

Permanent self-education, constant openness to the new lessons of experience, is one of the essential dimensions of the absolute priority of practice in Lenin's life. This – and above all the form of his self-education – created the unbridgeable gap between him and all empiricists or power-politicians. For he did not merely express his insistence on the category of the totality as basis and measure of politics polemically and pedagogically. The demands he made on himself were more stringent than those he made on his most valued collaborators. Universality, totality and con-crete uniqueness are decisive features of the reality in which action should and must be taken; the extent to which they are understood is therefore the measure of the true efficacy of any practice.

Of course, history may produce situations which contra-dict previously recognized theories. There may even be situations which make it impossible to act according to principles which are true and known to be true. For example, before October 1917 Lenin correctly predicted that, given the economic backwardness of Russia, a transi-tional form, such as what later became the NEP, would be indispensable. But the Civil War and intervention forced so-called War Communism on the Soviets. Lenin gave way to this factual necessity – but without giving up his theoretical conviction. He carried out as efficiently as possible all the dictates of War Communism the situation demanded, without – unlike most of his contemporaries – ever for a moment regarding War Communism as a genuine transitional form of socialism, and was absolutely determined to return to the theoretically correct line of the NEP as soon as the Civil War and intervention came to an end. In both cases he was neither an empiricist nor a dogmatist, but rather a theoretician of practice, a practitioner of theory.

Just as *What is to be Done?* is a symbolic title for his whole literary activity, so the theoretical basis of this work is a preliminary thesis of his whole world outlook. He established that the spontaneous class struggle of the strike, even if properly organized, only produces the germs of class-consciousness in the proletariat. The workers still lack 'knowledge of the irreconcilable opposition of their interests to the whole present political and social regime'. Once again, it is the totality which correctly points the way to the class-consciousness directed towards revolutionary practice. Without orientation towards totality there can be no historically true practice. But knowledge of the totality is never spontaneous, it must always be brought into activity 'from the outside', that is, theoretically.

The predominance of practice is therefore only realizable on the basis of a theory which aims to be all-embracing. But, as Lenin well knew, the totality of being as it unfolds objectively is infinite, and therefore can never be adequately grasped. A vicious circle seems to develop between the infinity of knowledge and the ever-present dictates of correct, immediate action. But this abstract–theoretical insolubility can – like the Gordian knot – be cut through practically. The only sword suitable for this is that human attitude for which once again we must refer to Shakespeare: 'The readiness is all.' One of Lenin's most characteristic and creative traits was that he never ceased to learn theoretically from reality, while remaining ever equally ready for action. This determines one of the most striking and apparently paradoxical attributes of his theoretical style: he never saw his lessons from reality as closed, but what he had already learned from it was so organized and directed in him that action was possible at any given moment.

I was lucky enough to witness Lenin at one of these innumerable moments. It was in 1921. There was a session of the Czech Committee at the Third Congress of the Comintern. The questions were extremely complex, and opinions irreconcilable. Suddenly Lenin walked in. Everyone asked him for his opinion of the Czech problems. He refused. He said he had tried to give the material proper attention, but such pressing affairs of state had intervened that he got no further than hurriedly leafing through the two newspapers he was carrying with him, stuffed in his coat pocket. Only after many requests did he agree to communicate at least his impressions of these newpapers. Lenin took them out of his pocket and began a quite unsystematic, improvised analysis, beginning with the leading article and ending with the day's news. This impromptu sketch became the deepest analysis of the situation in Czechoslovakia and the tasks of its Communist Party.

Obviously, as a man of readiness and constancy, in the reciprocal relation of theory and practice Lenin always opted for the priority of practice. He did this in striking fashion at the end of his major theoretical work of the first period of the Revolution, *State and Revolution*. This was written in hiding after the July days, but he was never able to complete the last chapter on the experience of the 1905 and 1917 Revolutions; the development of the Revolution did not allow him to do so. In the postscript he wrote: 'It is more pleasant and useful to go through the "experience of the revolution" than to write about it.' He said this with a deep sincerity. We know that he always exerted himself to make up for this omission. It was not he but the course of events that made it impossible.

There has been an important change in human attitudes over the last centuries: the ideal of the Stoic-Epicurean 'sage' has had a very stong influence on our ethical, political and social opinions, well beyond the limits of academic philosophy. But this influence was equally an inner trans-formation: the active-practical element in this prototype has become far stronger than in ancient times. Lenin's permanent readiness is the latest and till now the highest and most important stage of this development. The fact that today, as manipulation absorbs practice and the 'end of ideology' absorbs theory, this ideal does not stand very high in the eyes of the 'experts', is merely an episode, measured against the march of world history. Beyond the significance of his actions and his writings, the figure of Lenin as the very embodiment of permanent readiness represents an ineradicable value – a new form of exemplary attitude to reality.

Budapest, January 1967

Notes

1 (*page 16*) Lassalle, Bebel and Schweitzer were leading German socialists in the period before German unification in 1871.

2 (*page 16*) The Lassalleaner were the followers of Lassalle and constituted one current in the German socialist movement. They believed in achieving socialism through state-aided co-operatives and other reformist means, whereas their rivals, the Eisenacher, maintained a more militant programme. Wilhelm Liebknecht, the father of Karl, was a leader of the Eisenacher. In 1875 the Lassalleaner and the Eisenacher united to form the Social Democratic Party.

3 (*page 34*) The Otzovists, known also as 'Boycotters', were Bolsheviks who, in the period following the 1905 Revolution, opposed working in legal organizations – i.e. trade unions, co-operatives, etc. – demanded the recall of the Social Democrats from parliament, and argued that at a time of reaction the party should undertake only illegal work.

4 (*page 34*) The KAP (*Kommunistische Arbeiterpartei* – the (German) Communist Workers' Party) was founded in April 1920 following a split on tactics within the German Communist Party (KPD). The KAP stood for 'direct' action, accusing the KPD leadership of parliamentarism and passivity. Lenin gave his views on the split in Chapter 5 of '*Left-Wing' Communism, an Infantile Disorder*.

5 (*page 42*) With this term Lenin made a connexion between the theory of imperialism – expounded particularly by Rosa Luxemburg – which made its collapse dependent on purely economic, objective factors and centred it in the imperialist countries, and the theory – also implicit in Rosa Luxemburg – that countries under the imperialist yoke would automatically be liberated after a socialist revolution in the imperialist heartland (see Lenin's article, 'A Caricature of Marxism – "Imperialist Economism" ', 1916).

6 (*page 42*) Kautsky's theory of Ultra-Imperialism predicted, in his own words, 'the joint exploitation of the world by internationally united finance capital in place of the mutual rivalries of national finance capitals . . .'. Lenin quoted this, and undertook a critique of Kautsky's position, in Chapter 9 of *Imperialism, the Highest Stage of Capitalism*.

7 (*page 42*) Anton Pannekoek was a Dutchman who had been active in both the Dutch and German Social Democratic parties before the

war. Subsequently he joined the KAP (see Note 4 above). He later became a leader of the Dutch Communist Party.

8 (*page 42*) *The Accumulation of Capital* (1913) was Rosa Luxemburg's main theoretical work, the *Juniusbrochüre* (1916) one of her most important polemics.

9 (*page 51*) Massive police repression was unleashed against the newly created Communist Party in the USA in late 1919 and 1920. President Wilson's Quaker Attorney-General Palmer organized armed raids which resulted in the arrest of 6,000 militants and all the leaders of the party. In Boston, the prisoners were marched in chains through the streets, as in ancient Rome.

10 (*page 54*) *Die Internationale* was a theoretical journal founded by Rosa Luxemburg in April 1915. The 'Gruppe Internationale' included Karl Liebknecht and the critic, historian, and biographer of Marx, Franz Mehring. Later it became the 'Spartacus League', the embryo of the German Communist Party.

11 (*page 66*) Otto Bauer was one of the leaders of the Austrian Social Democratic Party.

12 (*page 70*) The Socialization Commission in Germany was headed by Kautsky. Set up to appease the Left, it was blocked by the resistance of the civil service, against which it received no support from the Social Democratic government. Kautsky tendered its resignation in April 1919.

13 (*page 75*) By state capitalism, Lenin meant here the control by the workers' state of capitalist producers and traders, who were permitted to operate 'within certain limits' at the time of the New Economic Policy. He distinguished it sharply from 'the state capitalism which exists under the capitalist system when the state takes direct control of certain capitalist enterprises'.

14 (*page 83*) Following the Kapp Putsch – the attempted military coup carried out by the Freikorps and other troops in Germany, which was defeated after four days by a general strike – the trade union leader Karl Legien proposed an all-party 'Workers' Government' of trade unionists. The German Communist Party agreed to conduct only a propaganda – in other words, a 'loyal' and non-revolutionary – opposition to such a government, which in fact never came into being.

15 (*page 84*) In June 1919 an ultimatum – the Clemenceau Note – was sent to Bela Kun from Versailles demanding the withdrawal of Hungarian troops from Slovakia (occupied by the Hungarian Red Army after its successful counter-offensive against interventionist forces) in exchange for the withdrawal of Rumanian forces in the east of Hungary. Against opposition to his left, Bela Kun accepted the Note and the Hungarian Red Army withdrew. The Rumanian forces stayed put and were subsequently employed to crush the Hungarian Soviet Republic.